HOMESPUN MEMORIES *for the* HEART

More than 200 Ideas to Make Unforgettable Moments

Karen Ehman, Kelly Hovermale, & Trish Smith

Revell
Grand Rapids, Michigan

Published by Fleming H. Revell
a division of Baker Publishing Group
P.O. Box 6287, Grand Rapids, MI 49516-6287

Printed in the United States of America

Library of Congress Cataloging-in-Publication Data
Ehman, Karen, 1964–
    Homespun memories for the heart : more than 200 ideas to make unforgettable moments / Karen Ehman, Kelly Hovermale, and Trish Smith.
        p.   cm.
    Includes index.
    ISBN 0-8007-5983-4 (pbk.)
    1. Family—Religious life—Handbooks, manuals, etc. 2. Family recreation—Handbooks, manuals, etc. 3. Amusements—Religious aspects—Handbooks, manuals, etc. 4. Entertaining—Planning—Handbooks, manuals, etc. I. Hovermale, Kelly, 1963–   II. Smith, Trish, 1969–   III. Title.
BV4526.3.E36 2005
249—dc22   2004025839

*"They will celebrate your abundance and joyfully sing
of your righteousness."*

PSALM 145:7

To those women who have shown us the importance of building memories:

Karen—To my mother, Margaret Patterson, for the dozens of cakes lovingly baked, the scores of gifts cleverly given, and the many sacrifices unselfishly made, it is to you I dedicate this book.

Kelly—To my mother, Kathy Ginter, for the investment you made in my life and the encouragement you graciously give to me as a wife and mother to my four precious children. Thank you for being not only my mother, but my mentor and friend.

Trish—To my aunt, Frances Underwood. From Easter baskets to Sunday dinners and family vacations, thank you for giving me an example to follow of how to celebrate every special day.

And to those with whom we continue to build these cherished memories, our families:

Todd, Mackenzie, Mitchell, and Spencer Ehman,

Greg, Steven, Austin, Jonathan, and Autumn Hovermale,

Doug and Zach Smith.

CONTENTS

1

Make Homespun Memories

. . . .

AN INTRODUCTION

*They will celebrate your abundant goodness and joyfully sing
of your righteousness.*

Psalm 145:7

Memories. The mere mention of the word conjures up images and emotions. For some folks, memories are the warm feelings they get as they remember Christmas mornings tiptoeing down the stairs still dressed in flannel pajamas, hoping to catch a glimpse of the treasures waiting below. For others, just the smell of a familiar fruit can evoke the memory of time spent with Grandma in the kitchen, waiting to sample her famous strawberry preserves. The sound of rain on the window can bring memories of a book read by flashlight under a makeshift blanket fort, an ordinary night turned into an adventurous yet safe time to treasure years later.

A scent, sound, sight, touch of something—most anything can trigger such recollections and transport you back to another time and place. Whether good or bad, these moments of the past—your memories—have shaped you into the person you are today.

Your Fingerprint on Celebrations and Memories

Now fast-forward to the present. Look at the people in your life: your circle of friends, immediate and extended family, even your casual acquaintances. Though your lives have converged at this point in time, the journeys that have brought you here are as unique as the whorls and loops of each individual fingerprint. You all have come from different places, experiences, and backgrounds, bringing to each new relationship a sample of what you've experienced along the way.

As coauthors and friends, Kelly, Karen, and Trish share lives that are a reflection of this truth. Each of them comes from a distinctive background, bringing to the table whatever memories and traditions they have experienced—sharing them with you here in the pages of this book. But look for that common thing they—like you in your circles—share.

KELLY'S STORY OF SIMPLE THINGS

Growing up in a small town, Kelly's life was simple, but the celebrations were rich—and these are what continue to sustain her in a life that can grow complicated and crazily busy.

One of her favorite celebrations was always the "Hanging of the Greens," a Christmas tradition in her small village church. Church members of all ages gathered for one evening to deck the halls with beautiful decorations, sing carols, and munch a tasty cookie or two. She remembers looking through the boxes of Christmas decorations that were pulled out of storage for just the right ones to take back to the Sunday school classroom.

There were yards and yards of glittery gold and silver tinsel, and old Christmas cards portraying the important scenes of the Christmas story. Long, tangled strands of tree lights with those large, old-fashioned colorful bulbs, and a well-worn, misshapen tree were ready to have little hands create on it a masterpiece of holiday beauty. Looking further she found an eclectic assortment of ornaments used throughout many a Christmas past. And it was always a treat to find just the perfect Christmas angel to don the treetop.

Meanwhile, the men from the church would bring in a real pine tree that seemed to touch the ceiling. Then the ladies busied themselves by hanging homemade ornaments that would symbolize the story of the very first Christmas. The highlight of the evening was seeing the nativity scene being assembled outside on the church lawn. Children gathered round, anxiously awaiting nightfall and the illumination of the baby in the manger.

"The best part was that my family lived across the street from the church," Kelly remembers. "I would often ponder the quietness of the snow-blanketed nativity scene as I looked out the window of my house."

These precious memories of Christmas have inspired Kelly to incorporate the tradition of a "Hanging of the Greens" in her home today. As she and her children decorate their little house in the suburbs of Detroit, they reminisce about each ornament—who gave or made it, when it was given, what was happening at the time, the first Christmas it hung on their tree. These decorating days are filled with Christmas music and the smell of warm gingerbread baking in the oven. And just as the nativity scene took center stage in the celebration in her hometown church, a miniature version now adorns the Hovermale living room. "My children's four little pairs of eyes look wistfully at the baby in the manger just as I did so many years ago," Kelly says. With celebrations, a family's love can be brought full circle through the generations.

These simple times and ordinary things bring Kelly great joy and comfort; she says the way they "just happened" encourages her that they can be recreated and reclaimed every year. "My mother never consciously had a plan. She didn't set out to make each day different and unique, but she did set aside the time to involve our family in those simple things that would create lasting memories."

The celebrations and memory-making activities seemed to come naturally to her. She never owned a planner like many moms use today, or went to conferences to hear speakers teach on building memories with your family. Certainly books on celebrations and memory making were few and limited back then. Living in a small rural town, she found that many resources and entertainment opportunities were unavailable. They simply relied on making memories around home as a family. Whether it was going ice skating down at the park on a brisk winter evening and returning home to mugs of hot chocolate and freshly baked cookies or making homemade ice cream on a warm summer day after swimming in the family's pool, these were the normal things they did to build memories.

Making memories for her children was always a part of her thinking. She had a mind-set of building memories that included most often the simple things in life. These are the memories Kelly wants her children to remember about their childhood—the simple things celebrated as a family.

KAREN'S STORY OF A CREATIVE MIND

Neither expensive gifts and elaborate celebrations nor grand family vacations made memories for Karen. In fact, she says, none of these things were part of her upbringing in any way. Out of necessity, her mother was forced to get creative when it came to making wonderful memories for her children.

As a single mother of two small children, Karen's mother lived on a budget so tight it squeaked. Her gifts on birthdays may have been the most inexpensive, but they were often the most clever.

"To this day I still think I might find something hidden in the breadbox on the morning of my birthday," Karen says, telling about scavenger hunts more fun than any one gift. There were always "just because" treats lovingly baked specifically for the return home from school on a rainy afternoon, or poems left on the table for encouragement the day of cheerleader tryouts or student council elections.

"She showed me that money is secondary to love and time together is more important than material trinkets," Karen says. "Today as I shop, plan, and celebrate with my own three children, so many of my mom's ways are now my ways. I scour garage sales and secondhand stores to find just the right gift—and God often puts the exact item in my path. Most recently it was a pair of nearly new cowboy boots for my young buckaroo, who was turning six in three weeks. 'That will be $2.98, please' was music to my ears!"

Today Karen's kids go on their own scavenger hunts, receive poems left on their pillows, and look forward to treats baked after a day of homeschool. "Am I turning into my mother?" Karen wonders. "I hope so! I consider that the highest of all compliments. All those years I was watching, seeing a mom who could take a meager paycheck and a simple idea and spin it into love and pure magic."

TRISH'S STORY OF FRESH STARTS

Not everyone has such pleasant memories of joyful holidays and beautiful birthdays. Trish experienced a stormy home life and mostly painful memories of a childhood vacant of celebration and peace.

A gift just for her, when she was sixteen and in a new living situation with an aunt, changed everything.

"I will never forget opening my door that Easter morning on my way to the kitchen to fix myself some breakfast," she says. "I never dreamt there would be a gift lovingly placed outside my bedroom door. I felt valued and special—all because of a small, simple basket of chocolates and candies given by my sweet Aunt Fran."

Aunt Fran had a knack for making simple things extraordinary beyond Easter too. Sunday dinner, in fact, was an event. Aunt Fran would get up early to prepare special recipes that would be ready and waiting for the family's return from church; these dinners set Sundays apart from the rest of the week. They were beautiful, extravagant in the love that prepared them, and made for a restful oasis from the hustle and bustle of school activities or work on weekdays.

The same love that went into Sunday dinners made family vacations an oasis for Trish. "After living with my aunt and uncle, for the first time I understood the anticipation of planning and packing and then the sometimes tedious time of traveling in the car—looking for ways to keep busy, ways to make the time go faster and the destination come quicker. But even those times of seeming boredom have turned into cherished memories of whispering with my sister in the backseat of a station wagon, sharing plans and thoughts, dreams and wishes."

As an adult with her own family, Trish says she finds her eyes turning to her teen past, looking for traditions and routines from her aunt and uncle to incorporate into her own home. "In many ways I want my home to be very different from the one into which I was born, but looking back to my aunt's example, I feel encouraged to build significant memories with my husband and son—to turn the tide from what I experienced early in life. It's never too late to begin building wonderful memories with your friends and family. You can always start fresh and make memories now to cherish in years to come."

WHAT'S YOUR STORY?

So, what about you? Where did you come from? What eyes are now upon you? How can you help point those eyes to God?

By making the time and effort to create celebrations and build memories, you show those around you how much you love life and people. You also honor the God who created all. You'll find tangible benefits too, as celebrations help you connect with your loved ones and make your home an inviting place to be—where family and friends will want to return after time away at school or work. After all, it isn't the celebration itself that's important but the people with whom we share it. In an often crazy, chaotic, and de-

CELEBRATIONS IN THE BEGINNING

Did you know that party-making, festivals, and days of thanksgiving are as old as Moses? In fact, they're actually as old as God! The God of Israel carefully instructed His people to spend time feasting and celebrating. In addition to a weekly time of worship on the Sabbath, God outlined nineteen feasts in the Old Testament—special times for remembering all He had done for them in times past and His promise to always deliver and sustain His people. Take a look at celebrations *a la* God and think of ways you might remember these celebrative roots of our faith:

■ **Passover** (Lev. 23:5): A celebration of God sparing the lives of the firstborn sons of Israel during the plagues in Egypt (see Exod. 12:1-13). This feast reminded the Israelites of God's deliverance. Still celebrated today, Passover begins in April (consult a calendar for the exact dates) and lasts for eight days. Families gather and celebrate with elaborate meals called *seders*.

■ **The Feast of Unleavened Bread** (Lev. 23:6-8): This feast commemorated the Israelites' exodus from Egypt (Exod. 12:31-42), reminding the people that they had left their old way of life behind and were beginning a new life. Celebrated directly after Passover, today these two feasts are often treated as the same festival.

■ **The Feast of the Firstfruits** (Leviticus 23:9-14): This celebration required the people to give back to God from the firstfruits of their harvest. It is a reminder that God provided the sun and rain needed to grow the crops.

■ **The Feast of Weeks** (Lev. 23:15-22): This feast celebrated a bountiful harvest and honored the One who had provided the harvest. Now called *Shavuot*, this celebration also commemorates the giving of the Ten Commandments to Moses and is observed exactly seven weeks after Passover.

■ **The Feast of Trumpets** (Lev. 23:23-25): On the first day of the seventh month, this feast was a time of rest and offering to God. Today, Jewish tradition tells us that *Rosh Hashanah* commemorates God's creation of the world.

■ **Day of Atonement** (Lev. 23:26-32): This feast celebrated restoration between God and Israel. The people's sin was removed, and they could have renewed fellowship with the Lord. Known as *Yom Kippur*, this is the most sacred of the Jewish holidays.

■ **The Feast of Tabernacles** (Lev. 23: 33-43): This celebration commemorated God's provision and guidance for His people as they wandered in the desert. The festival of *Sukkot*, as it is known today, is named for the huts that the Israelites lived in during their wanderings.

manding world, the joy of the celebrative home can help others feel secure and sheltered, valued and loved. In a world of strangers and oft-cruel pressures, the celebrative home says, "This is where you belong; this is where you can just be."

Many of the ideas presented here involve children. Because we are moms with young children at home, our thoughts naturally turn to including our kids in traditions and celebrations. But if you don't have children or your kids have already left the nest, you can adapt the kid-friendly ideas for your grandchildren, nieces and nephews—even the neighbor kids. Whether you're single or have a family of your own, you can begin to celebrate important holidays and events with your co-workers, neighbors, family, and friends, reaching out with Christ's love to those around you.

Don't limit these special times to those who reside within your four walls. Both holidays and seemingly ordinary days are perfect opportunities to reach out to those with whom your life naturally intersects. Not everyone comes from a place of comfort or a life filled with joy. Perhaps it is the widow down the street facing her first year alone or the neighborhood child often home by herself while her single parent is at work struggling to make ends meet. How can you make these people feel that same sense of belonging? How about making them a part of your celebrations or perhaps taking your show on the road? Deliver a "party in a box" to that lonely neighborhood child on his birthday—complete with a cake, a few presents, and of course party blowers and confetti. This simple gesture could brighten his entire week. How about a hot casserole shared with that widow from your church, carefully timed to be delivered just as the fallen leaves fill her front yard? Place a "Happy Fall" bouquet of wildflowers on her kitchen table to brighten her life in the days to follow. Take your rakes along too, and leave her with not only a clean yard but a thankful heart and glad smile as well.

When Moments Turn to Memories

Simple gestures. Small acts done with great love. These things last beyond a moment. Eyes are watching and learning from you.

It's our hope that within the pages of this book you will find many ways to celebrate all through the year. Whether it is a holiday, a holy day, or just a daily day with those you love, ideas are given designed to encourage, cheer, and spoil. From complete party theme ideas and ways to mark a spiritual milestone to holiday and seasonal ideas centered on a work of literature, we hope to give you the tools to make wonderful memories for those in your life.

Like the quilting bee of old where each brought to the table her simple scraps and strong thread, we've collected pieces of ideas from women both far and near. We've stitched them together here using the thread of our common love for our friends and families. The result, we hope, is an array of ideas, a tapestry of tales stretched out before you to see and to use. Use this volume as a resource, a springboard for celebrating as each page of your calendar is turned anew. And we pray that those who are now watching you will feel loved and included and will be ever so gently pointed to the One who gives us the reason to celebrate the very breath of life so graciously given each day.

THE SOURCE OF JOY

As children of God we have reason to celebrate every day, every moment—not just the major holidays when banks and the post office close. Copy the great reminders below on slips of paper to tuck into your pocket for days when you need a divine boost.

God is lovingly pursuing you. He wants you to be a part of His family, and He's building a home just for you. Luke 19:10 says, "For the Son of Man came to seek and to save what was lost." In Matthew 14:2 Jesus promises, "In my father's house are many mansions. . . . I go to prepare a place for you" (KJV).

You belong to God's family once you accept His love and by faith accept Jesus as the sacrifice for your sins. "You are all sons of God through faith in Christ Jesus," Galatians 3:26 promises.

You have the promise of divine guidance and comfort from the Holy Spirit, who lives in all who accept what Jesus accomplished for the world by sacrifice on the cross. "Because you are sons, God sent the Spirit of his Son into our hearts. . . . So you are no longer a slave, but a son; and since you are a son, God has made you also an heir," Galatians 4:6–7 says.

Nothing can remove you from God's hand, once you are in His family—not anything you do or fail to do. "Now a slave has no permanent place in the family, but a son belongs to it forever," the Scripture says in John 8:35–36. "So if the Son [Jesus] sets you free, you will be free indeed."

We have every reason to celebrate every day. As 2 Corinthians 9:15 puts it, "Thanks be to God for his indescribable gift!"

2

CELEBRATE THE NEW: SPRING

. . . .

MUD PUDDLES AND GALOSHES, PASSOVER AND PRAYER

See! The winter is past; the rains are over and gone. Flowers appear on the earth; the season of singing has come.

SONG OF SONGS 2:11–12

Almost gone are the cold, barren days of winter. Galoshes and umbrellas will soon replace mittens and scarves, and instead of building snowmen, children will make mud pies and splash in mud puddles. Look closely and you'll find signs of new life all around you: purple crocuses peeking their heads out of the newly thawed ground, robin redbreast resuming a familiar place under the porch eaves, tiny buds bursting forth into great green leaves that will soon offer shade from summer's heat.

Just as nature undergoes the process of rebirth and renewal, why not use this season to turn over a new leaf with those you love? This chapter blooms with fresh, bright ideas for making memories and celebrating the wonders of God's creation.

Luck O' the Irish

You won't need Irish genes or luck (but prayers—definitely!) to make St. Patrick's Day a winner in your home. Try the following ideas.

FOLLOWING THE CHARM OF THE IRISH

If there are little ones in the house, let them know that a leprechaun or two may have paid a visit during the night. Sprinkle some Lucky Charms cereal down the hallway and out the front door and watch their delight as they follow the trail and marvel and wonder about the little people. For fun, watch together the old Disney film *Darby O'Gill and the Little People.*

GREEN EGGS AND HAM . . . AND MILK . . . AND . . .

Linda Dawson of Savage, Minnesota, is one-half Irish and for St. Patrick's Day serves her kids a green breakfast. Simply adding green food coloring to the pancake batter or scrambled eggs can help turn your breakfast a lovely shade of leprechaun green. Or perhaps in the middle of the night that same food coloring can mysteriously turn your entire gallon of milk bright green, further proof that you may have had an Irish visitor while you slept. Linda also dyes carnations by putting them in a vase of water with a few drops of green food coloring added. By the end of the day the carnations start to turn green. The kids love to see how the flowers drink up the green water. Note: for the best color, make sure to give the carnation a fresh cut before placing it in the colored water.

AN IRISH TOUCH

Look for a tape or CD of real Irish folk music to play during the family supper. Get out a map, globe, or atlas and show the children where Ireland is.

Check out a library book that tells the story of Saint Patrick and his role in the spread of Christianity. To prepare your children for this special day, begin reading on March 1. We recommend *Saint Patrick: Pioneer Missionary to Ireland* by Michael J. McHugh, available from Christian Liberty Press (online at http://ebiz.netopia.com/clpress/). Each chapter ends with questions to promote conversation. Talk about the people in your life and with whom God may want you to share His message of hope and salvation.

For a festive centerpiece, purchase a shamrock plant at a local nursery. They are very easy to grow indoors, even if you don't have a green thumb! Legend indicates that Saint Patrick used the shamrock as a metaphor to explain the Trinity, with the three leaves representing the Father, Son, and Holy Spirit.

THE MEAL TO MAKE THE DAY

For supper, make a meal of Oven Irish Stew, Irish Soda Bread, and Mint-Chocolate Brownies. After the meal, crank up the Irish music, push back the chairs, and let the kids dance a jig. Brave adults may join in too. "Erin go braugh!"

Oven Irish Stew

$1\frac{1}{2}$ pounds eye of round beef, cubed
1   28-ounce can diced tomatoes
2   celery ribs
1   pound bag of baby carrots
3   chopped onions
3   pounds red potatoes, peeled and cubed
1   teaspoon salt
$\frac{1}{2}$ teaspoon pepper
1   teaspoon garlic powder
$\frac{1}{4}$ cup dry minute tapioca
1   tablespoon sugar
1   10-ounce bag frozen peas

Mix all ingredients in a large roaster pan. Cover and bake at 275 degrees for 5 hours. Serves 6–8.

Variation: To make in a slow cooker, place ingredients in crock, cover, and cook 4–6 hours on high heat or 8–10 on low heat.

Irish Soda Bread

4   cups bread flour
$\frac{1}{4}$ cup sugar
1   teaspoon salt
$1\frac{1}{2}$ teaspoons baking powder
$\frac{1}{4}$ cup butter

$1\frac{1}{3}$ cups buttermilk
1   egg
1   teaspoon baking soda
2   cups golden raisins

In a large bowl, mix dry ingredients. Cut in the butter with a pastry blender or large fork. In a small bowl, beat together buttermilk, egg, and soda. Add raisins. Stir into flour mixture until moistened.

Turn the dough onto floured board and knead gently. Form into a large round loaf and place on a greased cookie sheet. Cut a cross about 1½ inches deep in the top of the loaf.

Bake at 375 degrees for 45 minutes. Cover with foil and bake 15 minutes longer until the loaf sounds hollow when tapped.

Cool for 10 minutes. Serve with lots of butter to melt in your mouth.

Mint-Chocolate Brownies

BROWNIES:

1½	cups butter, melted
3	cups sugar
2	teaspoons vanilla
5	eggs
2	cups flour
1	cup cocoa
1	teaspoon baking powder
1	teaspoon salt
24	small chocolate-mint patties

FROSTING:

8	ounces cream cheese, at room temperature
¼	cup butter, at room temperature
2–3	tablespoons milk
16	ounces confectioner's sugar
2	teaspoons vanilla
	a few drops green food coloring

Mix all brownies ingredients except mints together in a large bowl just until moistened. Reserve 2½ cups mixture and spread the rest in a greased 9-by-13-inch pan. Place patties on top and then spread the remaining mixture on last. Bake at 350 degrees for 45–50 minutes. Allow to cool.

In a medium bowl, blend frosting ingredients together until creamy. Spread on cooled brownies.

Spring Has Sprung

For a sweet surprise when the children awaken on March 20, the first day of spring, give baskets that celebrate the season. They can be as elaborate or simple as you like. There are so many pretty and fun candies out this time of year in the shapes of chicks, lambs, bunnies, and birds—place some in a basket. (Don't forget those yellow marshmallow peeps, nutty and nostalgic.)

Include other springtime favorites: a new kite, ball, Frisbee, or jump rope. Tuck in a gift certificate for an anticipated warm-weather activity like putt-putt golf or horseback riding. Tie on a copy of the tag from page 176 that features Song of Songs 2:11–12: "See! The winter is past; the rains are over and gone. Flowers appear on the earth; the season of singing has come."

Even a note in lieu of candies and gifts makes a child feel special and helps you and your children celebrate the wonder and beauty of spring.

SOME BUNNY LOVES YOU

These edible treats are another way for all those little bunnies in your home to enjoy the first day of spring at lunch or dinner. You'll need:

- canned pear halves
- banana slices cut lengthwise, sprinkled with lemon juice so they won't turn brown
- lettuce

- raisins
- long, thin carrot sticks
- cottage cheese

Place a leaf of lettuce on each plate. On the lettuce place a pear half, core side down. Add banana ears. Add carrot-stick whiskers. Cut little holes in the pear and insert raisins for eyes, nose, and mouth. Finally, using a small spoon, place a ball of the cottage cheese at the bottom of the pear as a fluffy cotton tail.

WATCH A CATERPILLAR WITH WONDER

This darling activity keeps little hands busy and feeds the mind and imagination. Read *The Very Hungry Caterpillar* by Eric Carle, then make a caterpillar the kids can watch grow.

Cut off a leg of pantyhose, about 24 inches long, leaving on the toe. In a bucket, make a mixture of four cups potting soil to one cup grass seed. Using a trowel, place enough of the mixture in the toe end of the nylon to make a ball about the size of a tennis ball. Twist the nylon and tie off the twisted end with string.

Repeat the process several more times, tying off each time to make the various sections of the caterpillar. End with a tight tie and clip off the remaining nylon.

With a low-temp hot glue gun, attach two pipe cleaners for antennae and two eyes purchased from a craft store along with a red felt mouth on the final section of the caterpillar.

Place the caterpillar on a tray or plate in a sunny location indoors. Water well and continue to keep relatively moist as the days progress. Stand back and wait for your little critter to sprout a cute coat of hair. You may need to use scissors to keep him looking trimmed and neat. When the kids at Trish's church tried this cute idea, it brought weeks of fun anticipation.

FIRST ROBIN DAY

The Davis family of Saint Johns, Michigan, has a fun family ritual that takes place each spring. Those of you living in an area of the country where the birds return from the South after the spring thaw each year might make this tradition one of your own!

The idea is a simple one: the person in the family who spies the first robin that has returned from the South is given a special prize or treat. It can be a consumable food item, or you might even get creative and find a robin figurine (call it your "bird of happiness"!) that's officially given to that person each year—along the same lines as a traveling trophy.

Now, the person must have a witness. No going out to get the mail and exclaiming, "I saw three robins in the front yard!"

The evening of the sighting, take the family out for ice cream as a foretaste of the warm months to come. Or you may want an easy, fun, hands-on edible for your family to make—like Robin's Nests.

Robin's Nests

1   12-ounce bag of peanut butter or butterscotch chips
1   large can of chow mein noodles
1   bag of assorted jelly beans or speckled malted balls that look like eggs

Slowly melt peanut butter or butterscotch chips in microwave or in a small saucepan on the stove over low heat, stirring often. Stir in chow mein noodles until they are coated with the melted chips. Have the children help you form "nests" out of the mixture. Place on wax paper to set up. Add jelly beans or malted balls for birds' eggs.

How Does Your Garden Grow?

Oh! The things which happened in that garden! If you have never had a garden, you cannot understand, and if you have had a garden you will know that it would take a whole book to describe all that came to pass there.

THE SECRET GARDEN
by FRANCES HODGSON BURNETT

These gardening ideas will delight one and all. Try putting one of these ideas to use in your garden this spring. They're sure to be a magnet for the neighborhood children.

CREATE A FAIRY GARDEN

Spring is a perfect time to delight both the young and young at heart with the making of a fairy garden. Karen's mother-in-love, Shirley, is famous for sparking her grandchildren's interest in this fun fantasy activity. Here's how you can make one too.

Dig up an irregularly shaped circular plot in a semi-shady place. Don't choose a square or rectangular bed. The birds are drawn to irregular borders (and perhaps fairies are too).

Plant all kinds of fairytale flowers and greens. Choose some miniature versions of bulbed plants such as tulips, daffodils, and hyacinths as well as other pint-sized varieties. Roses work well and can easily be found at most nurseries. Plant seedlings in such a manner as to leave room for a pathway leading to the main attraction of the garden—a fairy house!

Craft an A-frame house about two feet tall using three pieces of scrap plywood (any carpenter friend could locate some for you). Using one piece for each side and one for the bottom, make a triangular shape. The front and back of the structure remain open. If your fairies are the fancy type, glue cedar shingles in an overlapping manner on both sides of the roof. These can be found wherever dollhouse supplies are sold. Try a craft store.

Here is where you can get creative in the finishing of your fairy house. For a simple idea, paint it a pastel shade. If you want to try your hand at more elaborate painting, paint the background a light shade of cream or sage. Then paint on flowers, butterflies, and—for the really brave—a fairy or two.

Now gather twigs to fashion tables and chairs using a hot glue gun. If children are helping with this part, it's best to use a low-temperature glue gun. A large fresh leaf can serve as a tablecloth and dried mini-rosebuds serve as drinking cups for the fairies. Simply remove a few of the inner petals once the buds are dry, leaving a cup-shaped flower head.

To round out your garden, look for a fairy statue crafted from cement or resin, or perhaps metal wind chimes featuring fairies. Don't forget some wood chips down the path that leads to the fairy house.

To further add to the fun, check out the beautifully illustrated volume *The Complete Book of the Flower Fairies* by Cicely Mary Barker. A true classic, this edition contains all eight of the original flower fairy tales written in the 1920s and is sure to spark imagination and delight children of all ages.

Be sure to periodically check your fairy house for signs that it has had visitors in the night. Telltale signs are tipped over chairs and leaves blown in from the outside. Happy pretending!

BUILD A CLIMBING BEAN TEEPEE

Purchase eight or ten 6-foot bamboo poles, available at most gardening supply stores. Using twine, tie the poles together near the top. Then arrange the poles as you would for the frame of a teepee, pushing the bottom ends into the ground slightly to form a strong structure.

Next, plant seeds for any climbing plant around the outside of the edge of the frame—climbing beans work especially well, or try morning glories for a splash of color.

Finally, sit back and watch as the tiny green shoots begin to wind their way up the poles, filling in and making the perfect garden hiding place. Trish's niece, Hannah, loved peeping through the leaves in their teepee!

GROW A SUNFLOWER HOUSE

Using twine and stakes, lay out the dimensions of a playhouse in your yard. Include rooms, walls, and doorways. Then along the lines you have made, plant sunflower seeds, each just 6 inches apart. When the sunflowers have reached their full height, you have a house that will be the envy of all the neighbors . . . well, at least the littlest ones!

MAKE PETER RABBIT RIGHT AT HOME

> But Peter, who was very naughty, ran straightaway to Mr. MacGregor's garden and squeezed under the gate.
>
> THE TALE OF PETER RABBIT
> BY BEATRIX POTTER

For a fun springtime activity designed to get your children interested in digging in the soil (with Mom's permission!) and learning about gardening, plant a Peter Rabbit Garden!

Read aloud to your kids *The Tale of Peter Rabbit* by Beatrix Potter. Then trek outside, seeds and hoes in hand, to plant a replica of Mr. MacGregor's garden. Be sure to include many of the veggies that Peter ate when he snuck into the forbidden garden—cabbage, onions, parsley, radishes, and turnips. To insure that no little Peters spoil your perfect plot, plant marigolds around the edge. The rabbits aren't particularly fond of them. Or ask your hairstylist to save you some hair clippings to scatter around the perimeter of your garden. That is sure to keep the little buggers away! After your day of planting, enjoy some chamomile tea, either hot or cold, sweetened with a little honey, just as Peter did at the end of his day. His mother brewed some up for him to help settle his tummy after eating so many vegetables.

GROW VEGETABLE SOUP

For another gardening idea, look for the wonderful children's book *Growing Vegetable Soup* by Lois Ehlert. A father and child share the joys of planting, watering, and watching the plants grow. And once their harvest of tomatoes, corn, and potatoes is ready, they'll cook up a pot of the best veggie soup ever.

This book covers all aspects of gardening veggies, from preparing the tools and digging holes for the seeds to weeding, picking, washing, chopping, and cooking. Much to the delight of young and old, an easy and tasty recipe for vegetable soup is included on the flyleaf.

After reading the book, plant your own vegetable soup garden. This activity—half fun and half work—will keep your family working side by side throughout the summer.

When the harvest is ready, plan a trip to an antique shop to purchase a special soup pot in enamel or speckle ware. (Not just any old pot will do for your special soup!) Using the recipe from the book, make your soup and make a memory as your family shares it together. Then put your soup kettle away until next year when your family, like the characters in the book, gets to do it all again.

Fooled You!

Instead of the usual practical jokes that people play on each other on the first day of April, use this day to teach your children a spiritual lesson about "fools" and what the Bible has to say about them. We've provided a list of different verses that contain the word *fool* or *foolishness*. Try these simple ideas for an object lesson they'll never forget:

- **Take turns doing "foolish" things**— stand on your head, or make strange animal noises or silly faces.

- **Tell about your most embarrassing moment** and then go around the room for each person to share theirs too.

- **Ask what *wise* and *foolish* mean**, and ask everyone to share their thoughts. Then look up the definitions in the dictionary.

- **Using the chart provided for you on page 169, look up verses that contain the words *wise* or *foolish*.** Using the spaces provided, compare and contrast what it means to love wisdom or be a fool. Talk about how they can adapt these lessons to their lives.

- **Read the story in Matthew 7:24–27** about the wise and foolish men and where they built their houses. **Now build a house of cards.** See how simple vibrations can bring the whole thing tumbling down!

- **Sing the children's favorite**, "The Wise Man Built His House Upon the Rock."

Good resources for this study include *Proverbs for Parenting: A Topical Guide for Child Raising from the Book of Proverbs* by Barbara Decker; *For Instruction in Righteousness: A Topical Reference Guide for Biblical Child-Training* by Pam Forster; and two family- and child-oriented CDs, *Go to the Ant: Proverbs for the Family* by Judy Rogers and *The Wise Man Built His House* by Sacred Music Services.

Easter

The entire Easter season is a time of real celebration for the believer. From lessons about the Passover to Good Friday and Easter morning, bringing out the true meaning of Easter is so important in a world crying out for hope, grace, and redemption.

STIR THE SPIRIT

While many in our culture celebrate Easter with bunnies, chicks, eggs, and Easter baskets, you can teach your friends, family, and children about the risen Christ with these symbols and activities that invite spiritual discussion.

OUT OF THE BRICK OVEN

For a new twist on the traditional Passover meal, try making your own unleavened (pita) bread or serving lamb burgers! If making the bread, talk about how the Jewish people scoured the house getting rid of any leaven (yeast) that was found. They made and ate the bread in remembrance of Moses and the Jewish believers who had to quickly flee Egypt once Pharaoh finally let them go (Exod. 12:31–34). Because they had to leave so quickly, there was no time to wait for bread to rise! If you'd like to try your hand at the lamb burgers to give your family a taste, you may use store-bought pita bread instead.

Unleavened Bread

1 cup whole wheat flour	2 teaspoons oil
1/4 teaspoon salt	1/4 cup water
1 tablespoon butter or margarine	

Mix flour and salt together. With a fork, cut butter into flour mixture until crumbly. In a small bowl, mix oil and water together. Add to flour mixture and blend until it begins to leave the sides of the bowl.

Turn the dough onto a lightly floured surface. Knead for a minute or two. Add a small amount of flour and press dough flat with your hand. Roll out as thinly as possible. With a fork, make perforations in the dough. Bake on a lightly greased cookie sheet at 400 degrees for 8 minutes. Makes 4 pitas.

Lamb Burgers in Pita Bread

2½	pounds lean ground lamb		8	ounces feta cheese, crumbled
⅔	cup fresh bread crumbs		2	tablespoons fresh lemon juice
2	eggs, beaten		¼	cup chopped fresh parsley or cilantro
1	cup minced onions		2½	teaspoons salt
½	teaspoon minced garlic		1	teaspoon pepper

TO SERVE:

6 pitas, warmed • sliced tomatoes and red onions • crumbled feta cheese
peeled, chopped cucumbers • sour cream or plain, unsweetened yogurt

In a large bowl, combine all ingredients for burgers, mixing well. Cover and refrigerate for several hours or overnight.

Form the meat mixture into eight large patties. Fry in a nonstick pan in a little olive oil or grill over medium heat until the meat is no longer pink in the center.

Warm the pitas in foil in the oven at 250 degrees for 10 to 15 minutes. Cut each pita in half, crossways, forming two pockets. Cut the meat patties in half and place one inside each pita.

Add sliced tomatoes, onions, cucumbers, sour cream or yogurt, and feta cheese to each person's liking.

Resurrection Cookies

While serving as coeditors of a newsletter for at-home moms in the late 1990s, Karen and Kelly received this moving idea from a reader. The process of making these cookies and retelling the gospel story will make a lasting impression on a family. To make the resurrection story come alive, be sure to begin this recipe on Saturday night, right before Easter morning.

1	cup whole pecans	Bible
1	teaspoon white vinegar	wax paper
3	large egg whites	plastic bag with a zip closure
	pinch of salt	wooden spoon
1	cup of white sugar	masking tape

Preheat the oven to 300 degrees. Place the pecans in the bag and close. Read John 19:1–3. Let the children take on the role of the Roman soldiers by using the wooden spoon to beat the bag of whole pecans, breaking them into very small pieces while shouting, "Hail, Jesus! King of the Jews!"

Next, read John 19:28–30. When Jesus became thirsty He was given vinegar to drink. Have the kids smell the vinegar. Place it in a large mixing bowl.

Add the egg whites to the bowl. Eggs represent new life. Jesus willingly gave up His life to bring new life to us. Read John 10:10.

Read Luke 23:26–27. Give each child a tiny pinch of salt. Let them taste some and then brush the rest into the bowl. This represents the salty tears Jesus's followers shed.

The ingredients so far aren't very appealing. Egg whites are bland, vinegar is sour, and the salt isn't good by itself. Now comes the sweet part of the story! Jesus died because of His love for us! Dump in one cup of sugar as you read Psalm 34:8 and John 3:16.

Beat with a mixer on high speed for 12 to 15 minutes until stiff peaks are formed. The whiteness represents the purity of those who have been cleansed from sin. Read Isaiah 1:18.

Gently fold in the pecans. Drop heaping teaspoons of the batter onto a cookie sheet lined with wax paper. Read Matthew 27:57–60. Each mound represents the rocky tomb where Jesus's body was laid.

Read Matthew 27:62–66. Jesus tomb was sealed tightly shut. Place the cookies into the oven, close the door, and turn off the oven. Give each child a piece of masking tape and have them help seal the oven shut.

Now it's bedtime. Your children may feel sad to leave the cookies in the oven overnight, just as Jesus's followers were sorrowful when the tomb was sealed shut. While tucking the kids in, read John 16:20–22.

On Easter morning, open the oven and remove the cookies. Notice the cracked surface. Take a bite. The cookies are hollow! On the first Easter morning, the disciples were amazed to find the tomb open and empty. Read Matthew 28:1–10.

Finish with prayer, thanking God for His incredible plan of salvation.

MAKE SENSE OF THE STORY

By Sight—Eyeing Heaven

Before leaving for church on Easter morning, let each family member release a helium balloon (purple or pink) into the air as you sing your favorite Easter song, maybe "Christ the Lord Is Risen Today!" This can be a powerful visual reminder that Jesus has risen.

By Taste—Make 'Em a Cake

Using a cake mold in the shape of a lamb, bake a lamb cake to represent that Jesus is the Lamb of God (John 1:29). Or bake a cake in the shape of a cross. Just bake a cake in a 9-by-13-inch pan. When cooled, invert on a tray. Cut out a cross shape. Discard the rest of the cake or save for another use. Frost and enjoy!

By Scent—Show the Easter Lily

Another children's book is *The Parable of the Lily* by Liz Curtis Higgs. This is a story of a little girl who receives a present and is disappointed because it is not a toy or a doll. So she discards the box down in the cellar. On her way to the garden to gather flowers for Easter morning, she passes the cellar and discovers that her gift is alive. It is a beautiful lily.

By Illustration— Stories and Symbols

For a cute Sunday school treat, place jelly beans of the colors listed in the poem on the tag of page 176 in a cellophane bag and tie shut with curling ribbon. Include a copy of this tag that illustrates a clever way to share the salvation message using the different colors of the jelly beans.

While decorating Easter eggs, read the book *The Legend of the Easter Egg* by Lori Walburg. This beautiful book tells the story of Jesus's resurrection and the meaning of new life through the symbol of the Easter egg.

Resurrection Eggs are a set of plastic colored eggs that tell the Easter story with small toys and symbols found in each of the twelve eggs. Sets are available through FamilyLife, a division of Campus Crusade for Christ, at 1-800-FL-TODAY or online at www.fltoday.com. They include a step-by-step discussion guide and activities to make the lessons come alive in the eyes of a child.

By Sound—Make Music for Their Ears

On Easter morning, wake your kids to the sound of a recorded song or hymn that tells of the wonder-

AT OUR HOUSE

Reclaiming Easter

As a young mother, I feared our children would grow up in a society where the celebration of Christ's birth took a backseat to Santa, and the observance of His death and resurrection was reduced to a glorified celebration of spring. My husband and I determined early on that we would swim against the tide of our culture and focus our efforts instead on the biblical truths of these holidays. The result has been some wonderful, Christ-centered family traditions. Here is a favorite Easter one:

On Good Friday we reflect on the magnitude of Christ's death. From noon until 3:00 p.m., all activity ceases. Little ones nap. The older children and I watch the *Jesus* video put out by Campus Crusade for Christ (available by calling 1-800-827-2788). It was filmed at over two hundred locations in Israel, and every word is taken directly from the Gospel of Luke.

In the evening, Dad leads us in another reflective activity. We have a makeshift cross ready. This can easily be made from two pieces of two-by-four wood or some large branches of a tree nailed together. For even greater effect, save the real tree you used for Christmas—and use it to make your cross. This helps children to see that the same baby Jesus whose birth we celebrate at Christmas grew up to be the Savior who died on the cross.

After the family is gathered, we read 1 John 1:5–2:2 and talk about how the sins we commit, the wrong things we do every day, are what nailed Jesus to the cross. Each person present quietly writes a sin they have been struggling with on a slip of paper. Those too young to write may draw pictures or have a parent help.

We play a song that helps to convey this message, such as "Feel the Nails" by Ray Boltz. As the song plays, each one then takes a turn nailing his or her sin to the cross. We leave the cross up in a prominent place until Easter morning, when the nails and papers will have been removed (don't forget to do this after the children have gone to bed!) and instead a length of purple cloth appears draped over the shoulders of the cross.

He is risen and our sins are forgiven!

Karen

ful resurrection of our Lord. "Celebrate Jesus, Celebrate" by Don Moen makes an excellent choice, as do favorite renditions of old gospel hymns such as "Christ the Lord Is Risen Today" or "Low in the Grave He Lay."

When the children come to the kitchen table for their breakfast (complete with hot cross buns, simply use your favorite sweet dough recipe, shaping the rolls in balls. When baked and cooled, adorn with a white cross using store-bought or homemade white icing), they'll spy their Easter baskets. Instead of baskets filled with ordinary Easter items, tuck in gifts to help your child grow spiritually throughout the year: a Bible, Bible highlighter, journal, Bible storybook (*Bizarre Bible Stories* by Dan Cooley is one all kids adore), a devotional, or Christian music CD or video. Don't forget some sweets! Many department stores carry milk chocolate and white chocolate crosses at this time of year. Be sure to include the tag on page 178 featuring the verses from Matthew 28:5–6.

EGGS: A SYMBOL OF SPRING—AND THE TRINITY

The egg is a traditional symbol of spring and has a special connection to the Easter season. Representing new birth and renewal, it is a fitting reminder of our Savior's victorious resurrection from the grave on Easter morning. In addition to this symbolism, an egg is also a great help in explaining to a child the meaning of the Trinity (Father, Son, and Holy Spirit). The three parts of the egg—the shell, the white, and the yolk—join to form one egg just as the Father, Son, and Holy Spirit are separate parts of the Trinity that join to form one whole.

Creating Blown Eggs

These delicate decorations will become a marvel and a treasure to your family, and the process isn't as difficult as you might think. Follow these steps:

- **Use a needle to poke a small hole** in the smaller end of an egg and a slightly larger hole at the opposite end.
- **Push the needle** in as far as you can and wiggle it around to puncture the membrane around the yolk.
- **Place your mouth over the small hole and blow out the egg** yolk and white through the larger hole into a bowl. (Save the yolks and whites to whip up an omelet or use in baking.)
- **Rinse and dry the hollowed egg shells.** Now the eggs are ready to color, but be careful, as they're fragile. If packed carefully, these will last for years.

Egg Decorating Tips

Use blown or hard-boiled eggs with any of the following decorating ideas.

- Use simple paper stickers to make designs on your eggs. Stick stars on your egg before coloring half an egg blue and the other half red. When dried, remove the stickers for a patriotic egg. Or try small round stickers—when these are removed from the colored egg, you'll have polka dots!

- Sit hard-boiled eggs in an egg carton. Drizzle rubber cement over the eggs in lines and squiggles. When rubber cement is dry, color the egg as usual. Let sit until color is dry. Then carefully rub off the rubber cement to reveal your designs.

- Make egg dye from crepe paper. Place several torn sections of crepe paper about 2 or 3 inches long in individual cups for each color. Pour boiling water over each cup. Let stand a few minutes. Then place eggs into the cups and let stand about 20 minutes or until desired shade is reached. Remove with a slotted spoon and allow to dry on paper towels or wax paper.

Nature's Best Dyes

To dye eggs in a unique way, use items commonly found in nature. First, put a single layer of eggs in a large saucepan and cover with water. Add a dash of vinegar. Add a natural dye substance from the list below. Bring water to a boil. Reduce heat and simmer for 20 minutes. Remove any natural substance left. Drain eggs. If you desire a darker color, let them stand in the natural dye overnight. Here are some coloring agents (and we're sure you can think of even more):

- blue: canned blueberry juice
- green: spinach leaves
- orange: onion skins
- red: beet juice or chopped fresh cranberries
- yellow: lemon peels or ground cumin
- beige: strongly brewed coffee or tea

THE COLOR OF FAITH

Just as you marvel at how certain elements can turn varying colors of the rainbow, you can marvel at the shades of grace that form our faith. Talk about these shades with those you love. Color one egg each of the following colors as you discuss what each represents and what it means to you.

White stands for purity and the grace Jesus Christ gives to us.

Purple represents the traditional color of royalty and reminds us that Jesus is the King of Kings.

Green signifies new life, now available to us through Christ Jesus our Lord.

Red (or deep pink) symbolizes the blood Jesus shed on the cross.

Black (mix all the colors together to obtain this color) is for the sins we've committed that are now forgiven in Christ.

Yellow is the Light of the World, Jesus, the Son of God.

Orange represents the beautiful sunrise on that first Easter morning.

After coloring your eggs as a family, put them in an Easter basket and take to a neighbor or an elderly couple. Have the children tell what each color represents. What a fun way to spread the Good News!

For a long-lasting egg decoration, carefully break a raw egg around the top. Remove the inner egg and wash out the shell. Set the egg shell in an egg carton with the open end facing up. Fill with dirt and sprinkle with grass seed. Finally, draw a cute little face on the front of the egg shell. Water and watch for your egg friend to sprout a new head of green hair.

And don't forget: never eat decorated eggs that have sat out at room temperature. They may not be safe. We like to dye a second batch and then store them in the fridge until right before Easter dinner. Happy coloring!

CELEBRATE A PASSOVER SEDER

Every year during Easter week, Debi Davis and her family in Saint Johns, Michigan, look forward to celebrating the Passover seder, which commemorates God's deliverance of His people out of slavery to the Egyptian pharaoh (see Exod. 6–12). The event is the root of our faith and one Jesus celebrated—and was ultimately part of, as Debi's version of the observance shows.

The word *seder* means *order*, as this celebration always follows the same order. Jewish families begin the Passover, which lasts seven or eight days, with a meal rich in symbols that teach the story of redemption. Only after God sent his Son, Jesus, did the true significance of these symbols become apparent. Find the richness of the celebration in this version. Gather:

- 2 candles
- 1 bunch parsley
- *matzoth* (or unleavened bread wafers)
- 1 leg of lamb, roasted, with the juices from roasting saved
- red grape juice
- salt water, place some in one bowl for each person
- 1 egg for each person, roasted by first hard boiling, then setting on the top oven rack for 15 minutes at 350 degrees. Let cool before serving.
- small bowl with a basting brush, filled with the lamb juices from roasting, at the father's place at the table
- one skull cap (or a folded handkerchief) for the father to wear
- Bible opened to Exodus 6, set near the candles

Set the table with your best dishes and goblets. Next to each plate place a small dessert plate and small bowl of salt water. On each plate place a roasted egg, sprig of parsley, and matzo wafer. Fill the goblets with grape juice. Set an extra place at the table to remain empty. Place candles at the center of the table with a box of matches.

30

For the supper prepare whatever recipes your family loves to complement the leg of lamb. Debi keeps it simple: redskin potatoes, asparagus, and cheesecake for dessert.

While an authentic Jewish Passover seder lasts a number of hours and uses up to twenty symbols, the Davis family has chosen the ten symbols best for teaching. The family uses a script like the one that follows, in which the cup is raised four times.

The father at the table puts on the skull cap, or a folded handkerchief, and calls the family to the table. He asks the mother to light the candles and invites her to read: "Blessed are you, O Lord our God, King of the Universe, who sanctifies us by your commandments and has ordained that we light the Passover candles."

The first cup is for sanctification. The father says, "Sanctification means to be set apart. In celebrating the Passover we remember Exodus 6:6, in which God says, 'I will bring you out from under the burden of the Egyptians.' God performed miracles to sanctify His people. As Christians we remember now the death of Jesus, which sanctifies us and frees us from sin."

Everyone drinks a small amount of juice. They dip their parsley sprig into the salt water and eat a bit while the father reads, "This reminds us of the tears shed by the Israelites when they were slaves in Egypt. Let's dip the parsley a second time to remember how God drowned the Egyptians in the Red Sea when He judged them for their cruelty."

The father invites all to break the *matzoth* into three pieces while he says, "When God told the Israelites He would let them go from Egypt, He also told them to make special cakes of unleavened bread, with no yeast. The Jews were to eat this *matzoth* with their coats on, which reminds us that the Jews were ready to leave at any moment. The Jews broke their *matzoth* into three pieces, hiding one in their napkin. As Christians, we understand the deep mystery behind this. The three pieces represent the three persons of the Godhead. The hidden piece represents Jesus, God's son, who was broken and buried." The father invites everyone to eat the *matzoth*.

The second cup is for the plagues. The father explains: "God poured out ten plagues on Egypt, the last of which convinced Pharaoh to let God's people go. As I list the plagues, dip your finger into your cup and let a small drop of juice drop onto your plate, remembering the suffering: blood, frogs, lice, flies on cattle, boils, hail, locusts, darkness, and death. Now let us lift our cups and drink, thanking God that He not only delivered Israel from the plagues but through Jesus has delivered us from the plague of sin." Everyone drinks a small amount of juice together.

The father invites everyone to peel their roasted egg and dip it into the salt water. He says, "The roasted egg reminds us of the hardness of Pharaoh's heart, and the salt water reminds us of the tears shed by the Israelites when he refused to let them go." Everyone eats as much of their egg as they wish.

The father takes the bowl with meat juice and acts out painting it on the doorway as the Jews painted blood on the doorposts. He says, "On the night of the final plague, God promised that He would visit every house to execute judgment and would take the life of every firstborn son—unless the family had marked the door of their house with the blood of a perfect lamb. If the family obeyed God and marked their door, He would 'pass over' that house; no one in that family would die." Everyone relaxes after this obedient act and dines on the Passover meal together.

The third cup is for redemption. The father says, "This cup reminds us of redemption and how the lamb offered on Passover was the price of deliverance for the nation of Israel. This third cup is what Jesus probably drank when He told His disciples, 'This cup is the new covenant in my blood, which is poured out for you,' as recorded in Luke 22:20." Everyone drinks a small amount together.

The fourth cup is for praise. The father says, "Many Jews to this day look forward to a golden age when the lion will lay down with the lamb, the world will be at peace, and the Messiah will reign from Jerusalem. As Christians, we know that this will occur only after Jesus returns. We drink the cup of praise together, in hope of His soon coming and the beginning of His kingly reign." Everyone drinks the remaining juice and proclaims, "Even so, come, Lord Jesus!"

The father now turns to the empty chair. "Who has noticed the extra place set at the table?" he asks. "According to Malachi, the appearance of the Messiah would be preceded by Elijah. Jews today symbolize this by setting an extra place and even going to search for Elijah. When he doesn't arrive, they say once again, 'Maybe next year he will come.' We set an extra place in joyous anticipation of the coming of our Lord and Savior, Jesus Christ."

May Day

Resurrect some of the fun and frolic of an old-fashioned celebration of May Day, the first day of—you guessed it!—May. Your celebration can be as simple as purchasing some baskets from a garage sale or secondhand store and filling them with fresh cut flowers. Attach a copy of the gift tag featuring the verse from Song of Songs found on page 176.

Now pile in the car and travel around your town leaving the baskets at the doors of those with whom you want to leave a pleasant surprise. Since you want this to be anonymous, ring the doorbell and run. (You may want to have your getaway car at an around-the-corner location so you can watch from there the smiles that unfold as the baskets are discovered.)

National Teacher Day

Can you recall a favorite teacher from grade school or high school and the way they encouraged and inspired you?

Since teachers impact our lives in so many ways, on the Tuesday of the first full week of May we celebrate National Teacher Day. Make it a tradition in your house to let these special people know just how much they mean to you and your children! Here are a few ideas for framing a class picture for those amazing folks who build up the lives of our children.

Chalk Up an Experience. Purchase an inexpensive frame from a discount store. Have a snapshot of the class enlarged to fit inside the frame. Have the kids help you break pieces of chalk into various smaller pieces. Then, with thick craft glue, adhere the pieces of chalk all the way around the outside of the frame for a cute look.

Button Up a Smile. Take a picture of your child holding a bright red apple. Place this in a small frame. With craft glue, place red buttons around the edge of the frame, completely covering the wood. Use a variety of sizes and hues for a one-of-a-kind gift. The teacher can simply slip in a favorite picture of her own in years to come.

A Pen for Your Thoughts. For an extra-special remembrance, take a more formal picture of the entire class. Have this enlarged to 5-by-7-inch size. Then have a large, ivory-colored mat cut at your local craft or framing store, maybe to fit an 11-by-14-inch frame. With a good-quality pen, have the students write on the mat a special sentiment for their teacher, along with their names. Or, if the students are very young, have the parents each write a short sentence conveying what it means to them to have such a special person in their child's life. In the bottom corner, date the picture. This present is guaranteed to make a lasting memory.

A New Kind of Apple for the Teacher. If you have a friend who homeschools, show up at her house on National Teacher Day with a tasty apple pie for her to enjoy with her students as they take a break from their studies.

HONOR TEACHERS

If the celebration of National Teacher Day or National Day of Prayer piques your interest in praying for your children's teachers on a more consistent, year-round basis, check out Moms In Touch.

This ministry has groups all around the world where two or more moms meet for one hour each week to pray for their children and their schools, teachers, and administrators. Moms, grandmothers, and others who are willing to pray for a specific school are all welcome! For more information or to see if there is a group already meeting near you, log on to www.momsintouch.org or email them at info@momsintouch.org.

National Day of Prayer

On our National Day of Prayer, then, we join together as people of many faiths to petition God to show us His mercy and His love, to heal our weariness and uphold our hope, that we might live ever mindful of His justice and thankful for His blessing.

PRESIDENT RONALD REAGAN, MAY 5, 1988

The first National Day of Prayer was proclaimed in 1775 by the Second Continental Congress. Throughout our nation's history, in times of want or plenty, at war or in peace, our people have turned to God in prayer. In the 1950s a Joint Resolution of the Congress requested the President to proclaim one day each year as a National Day of Prayer.

AT OUR HOUSE

Cinco de Mayo Party

Having lived in south Texas while in high school, I learned that Cinco de Mayo, May 5, celebrates Mexico's independence—and like a good neighbor, we can celebrate here in the United States too! Why not have some good ol' tortilla-popping, salsa-dipping fun, including a whack at a goody-filled piñata?

Our guests come with a Mexican dish to pass, ranging from homemade tortillas for quesadillas to fresh salsa, enchiladas, and a Mexican wedding cake. We pass out name tags—nobody is allowed to use their given name. Instead, for one night, we adopt traditional Mexican names. (Last year I resorted to pulling out my old high school yearbook to find more names.)

We decorate the picnic tables and backyard with colorful Mexican decor and have Latin music playing in the background. Prizes are given for the most authentic Mexican costume or for the best Mexican hat dancer. At the end of the night we blindfold the children and have them take a swing at a piñata filled with candy. *Olé!*

Dorothy Whitcomb, Saint Johns, Michigan

HOMEMADE FLOUR TORTILLAS

2 cups all-purpose flour

$^1/_2$ teaspoon salt

$^1/_3$ cup vegetable oil

$^1/_2$ cup warm water

Mix together and divide the dough into about 12 balls. Cover with plastic wrap and let rest for at least 30 minutes before rolling into thin circles and cooking in a lightly greased skillet, flipping after 3 minutes.

We now observe this special day on the first Thursday of May. Many churches across the country mark this event by holding prayer meetings for our nation, its leaders, and its armed forces. For more information, visit www.nationaldayofprayer.org.

To help the little—and not so little—ones in your home learn about the importance of prayer, try some of the following ideas:

- **Alphabet Prayers:** Take a letter at a time and pray about things that begin with that letter. Example: for "A," thank God for apples, airplanes, animals, etc.

- **Band-Aid Prayers:** When someone you know is sick, children can put a Band-Aid on their finger or arm to remind them to pray for that person. Talk about how God can heal all our hurts too. Read some Scripture about God's healing power, verses like Psalm 103:2–3, Psalm 147:3, and James 5:16.

- **Balloon Prayers:** Blow up a balloon and draw on it a picture of a mistake that you made. Tell God how sorry you are, and ask Him for forgiveness. Then pop the balloon. Pop! That quick, God forgives and forgets.

PRAYER PRETZELS

This fun, hands-on activity illustrates prayer to little ones in a way they'll not forget. Gather the needed pretzel ingredients, a Bible, and some paper and pencils. You'll need the dough prepared (mixed and risen) at the time you start the activity. You can do it by hand or in a breadmaker.

While the children roll out their pretzels, talk through the questions provided and make a Prayer List for the month. Look on page 170 for the copy-ready form. Display your Prayer List in a prominent place and watch to see how God answers those prayers. To make the dough:

```
1   cup minus 2 tablespoons warm water
2   cups bread flour
1/4 teaspoon salt
1/2 teaspoon sugar
1 1/2 teaspoons dry yeast
4   tablespoons coarse salt
1   large egg
```

If using a breadmaker, measure all ingredients except the egg and coarse salt into the bread pan. Select the "dough" setting and start machine. When the cycle is over, remove dough and proceed.

If mixing the dough by hand, place warm water (110–115 degrees) in a bowl with sugar. Sprinkle with yeast and let rest five minutes. Add salt and flour (but not coarse salt and egg) and mix well. Turn onto a lightly floured board and knead for 10 minutes. Place in a large, well-oiled bowl and cover with a towel. Let rise until doubled, about 1 1/2 hours. Punch down the dough and proceed.

Preheat the oven to 425 degrees. Divide dough into eight to twelve pieces. Let kids roll their dough into a rope a half-inch in diameter, working on a lightly floured surface. As they roll, read these verses and the corresponding questions:

- When do we pray? (Eph. 6:18; 1 Thess. 5:17)
- How do we pray? And how should we not pray? (Rom. 8:25; Heb. 11:6)
- For whom do we pray? (Matt. 5:44; Phil. 1:1–6; 1 Tim. 2:1–4)
- Where do we pray? (Matt. 6:6)

Now show the egg. Ask which part of the egg is the most important: the shell, the white, or the yolk? Talk about how if one of the parts were missing, it would no longer be an egg. If there were no shell, how could it hold together? If there were no white, how could you eat a fried egg? If the yolk were missing, scrambled eggs would be a white, messy goo! Relate this to the Trinity, pointing out how God is three in one: all three persons—the Father, the Son, and the Holy Spirit—must be present for God to be God. This triune God is the one who hears and answers our prayers.

Now break open the egg, place it in a small bowl, and beat it slightly. Place the kids' dough "ropes" on a well-greased cookie sheet. Have them fold the ropes in the traditional pretzel shape, much like hands folded in prayer. Brush the pretzels with the beaten egg. Have the kids sprinkle on the coarse salt. This is much like the shedding of our salty tears that may come when we are praying to God about a sad situation, such as when someone we love is very sick, or when we cry to God over a bad or wrong thing we've done for which we're truly sorry.

Bake the pretzels for 13 to 17 minutes or until lightly browned. While they are baking, use the certificate provided on page 170 to make up a prayer list of those people and situations that need your prayers. You may even have time to begin praying for those requests right now. Praying "popcorn prayer" style (see page 129) works well, with each one offering short sentence prayers as they come to mind and the adult closing out the time.

Don't forget to display your prayer list throughout the month and discuss the ways God is answering.

Ten Ways to Tell Mom
"I Love You"

Mothers love to receive gifts that are from the heart, especially on Mother's Day. However small and inexpensive, these are the gifts that show love like no other. Here are some ideas to celebrate the mother or mother-in-law (or mother-in-love—the ones you choose) in your life.

Take your mother out for lunch, dinner, or a cup of coffee, just the two of you, and reminisce about your youth. Using specific examples from your past, tell her what a wonderful mother she is and how you treasure your relationship.

Write and mail her a letter or poem from your heart, printed on some pretty stationery. It doesn't matter if the poem rhymes or even if your mother lives next door to you. Ladies love to get mail, and it will thrill her to read a special message from you. In this day of email, a handwritten letter will mean so much more.

Restore an old family photo and frame it to give her as a gift. Perhaps a picture of her own mother would be especially meaningful to her.

Make a garden stone with a special message on it or with your fingerprint or handprints. Just buy a patio square and use outdoor paint to create your gift. Spray with polyurethane to seal.

Make a video that highlights your family's life over the past year. End it with a Mother's Day message from you and the kids.

Write your father a thank-you note telling him how glad you are that he married your mother.

Buy a blank book or journal in which your mother can write her favorite memories. In advance, write some questions to cue her reminiscing: "How did you wear your hair when you were a schoolgirl? What was your favorite subject? Who was your best friend? Where were you when you got your first kiss? What favorite hymns and songs have you loved over the years and why? Who gave your first Bible to you? What is your idea of what heaven will be like?" In the very front of the book, write thoughtful messages to surprise your Mom. This is a gift she can in turn give you someday—a collection of priceless memories of her own.

Make a generational family gift. Mat and frame pictures of you, your mother, your daughter, and possibly your grandmother too.

Purchase a collage frame and fill it with pictures of some of your favorite times with your mom, both from when you were a child and some from your adult years. Under each picture, write a short caption about the time spent together. You can include pictures of your children as well.

Make a "Memorabilia Basket." Line a pretty basket with lace or material. In it you could have silk or dried flowers, your parents' wedding photo and wedding invitations, or some items from your youth—perhaps your first Bible, a piece of special jewelry, your scout medals, an I.D. or charm bracelet . . . the possibilities are endless!

Memorial Day

Once upon a time our veterans were treated with respect and reverence. Schoolchildren happily recited the Pledge of Allegiance and leapt to their feet with hand held solemnly over their hearts as the American flag passed by. Unfortunately, Memorial Day in our time means little more to most children than a day outdoors to grill hamburgers and take a break from their schoolwork. However, we can still capture some of that spirit of patriotism with some careful planning and fun activities as we teach our young children the true meaning of Memorial Day.

Talk with your children about those soldiers who died defending our country or fighting for freedom around the world. See if you can come up with the names of any people in their life who have served in any branch of the armed forces—the army, navy, air force, marines, Coast Guard, or National Guard. Have them write a letter of appreciation to one of them thanking them for their service to their country. A phone call works well too.

Take a stroll through a public cemetery with paper and pen in hand. Record the names and dates of anyone you find who died during a war. If you are able to locate any headstones for soldiers who died during wartime, do a Web search to see if you can find out anything about the soldier who died.

Make one or both of the following recipes from the Civil War era. Do it as and with a prayer.

Hardtack

Soldiers in the Civil War existed on very little food rations. Many times all they had was coffee to drink and hardtack to eat. Whip up a batch of this bland, cracker-like staple of the Civil War.

For lunch on Memorial Day, make this your family's meal. After having only coffee to drink—with no cream and sugar—and hardtack to eat for lunch, that traditional Memorial Day cookout dinner will taste like a gourmet feast!

- 5 cups flour
- 1 cup water
- 1 tablespoon salt

In a medium bowl, mix all ingredients thoroughly until the dough is no longer sticky, adding more flour as necessary. Knead dough and roll out on a well-floured surface until it is a half-inch thick. Cut dough into 3-by-3-inch squares and poke all over with a fork to make holes, saltine cracker style.

Preheat oven to 425 degrees. Place dough squares on a lightly greased cookie sheet. Bake for 20–30 minutes until lightly golden brown. Cool and store at room temperature in a covered container, or wrap in a handkerchief as the soldiers did.

Civil War Gingerbread

For a more palatable dining experience, try this recipe for Civil War Gingerbread. Serve with a dollop of sweetened whipped cream for a real treat!

Preheat oven to 350 degrees. In a medium bowl, mix together:

2³/₄	cups all-purpose flour
2	teaspoons baking powder
¹/₂	teaspoon ground cloves
¹/₂	teaspoon baking soda
³/₄	teaspoon ground ginger
2	teaspoons ground cinnamon

IN A LARGE BOWL, CREAM:

³/₄	cup sugar
²/₃	cup shortening
1	teaspoon salt

BLEND INTO CREAMED MIXTURE:

1	cup molasses
2	eggs

Add flour mixture to the creamed mixture alternately with 1 cup hot tap water, blending well. Pour into a well greased and floured 9-by-13-inch pan. Bake for 40 to 50 minutes or until a cake tester inserted near the center comes out clean. Enjoy!

3

CELEBRATE GOLDEN DAYS: SUMMER

· · · · · · · · · · · · ·

BICYCLES AND BERRIES, FIREWORKS AND FLOWERS

*Consider how the lilies grow. They do not labor or spin. Yet
I tell you, not even Solomon in all his splendor was dressed
like one of these.*

LUKE 12:27

Summer is a perfect season to spend time with friends and family, celebrating God's beautiful creation. His hand is seen in the flowers blooming, the sunlight pouring down, the nourishing rain, the starlit nights. This chapter's indoor and outdoor activities range from patriotic celebrations to formal garden parties and informal berry-picking with your kids—all the right stuff to make the most of this scenic season with its long, sunny days and golden memories waiting to be made.

Salute the Flag

Who knew what would come from a sister in Christ sewing a flag for a church friend? History tells us it's exactly from such humble origins that the American flag was created. In June 1776, George Washington approached a seamstress who attended church with him and asked her to sew the first flag.

Betsy Ross did, using a pattern probably designed by a delegate to the Continental Congress, and the original flag began to wave. It had thirteen red stripes on a white background and thirteen stars in a circle on a blue background. Simple but striking, this flag was officially adopted by the Continental Congress on June 14, 1777, and is known, with later variations, around the world. We celebrate Flag Day every June 14.

Invite your loved ones into a discussion of what they would have done if someone in church asked them to sew a flag. Then stoke your creativity to make some Flag Day decorations and try these activities:

- Get out some paper and sketch the symbols you'd use if you were designing the flag. What do you want to say visually? What symbols and colors would you use and why?

- Have a sewing lesson. Use muslin as a background and with a simple running stitch add red stripes, a blue background in the upper left corner, and white stars on the blue.

- At your local library, check out a book on the life of Betsy Ross. Try *Betsy Ross: Designer of Our Flag* by Ann Weil, part of the Childhood of Famous Americans series. Discover in more detail her role in the creation of the first flag.

- Talk over flag etiquette with your kids. See page 53.

- Say the Pledge of Allegiance and mean it:

    "I pledge allegiance to the Flag
    of the United States of America
    and to the Republic for which it stands,
    one nation under God, indivisible,
    with liberty and justice for all."

- Make a Stars and Stripes Tart, a wonderful and refreshing dessert for Flag Day or your Fourth of July picnic that looks like the American flag. Stick a candle (or sparkler) in it and sing "The Star-Spangled Banner."

Stars and Stripes Tart

CRUST:

- 1 cup butter, softened
- 1/4 cup sugar
- 2 1/2 cups all-purpose flour
- 1/3 cup milk

FILLING:

- 1 1/2 packages light cream cheese, softened
- 1 cup powdered sugar
- 1 teaspoon vanilla (or almond) extract

TOPPING:

- 1/2 pint blueberries
- 1 pint strawberries, hulled and sliced
- 1/3 cup apple jelly, melted

Preheat oven to 400 degrees. In a large bowl, beat butter and sugar until light and fluffy. Add flour and milk and beat on low until well mixed. Press dough on bottom and a half-inch up sides of a 9-by-13-inch pan. Prick with a fork and bake 14 to 18 minutes until lightly browned. Cool.

Combine filling ingredients and mix at medium speed until light and fluffy. Spread over cooled crust.

Refrigerate at least two hours. Just before serving, arrange fruit to resemble the American flag. (With pan horizontal, arrange blueberries in upper left corner in a rectangle for stars. Place strawberries in rows for stripes.) Brush fruit and filling with melted jelly.

Dear Old Dad

Honor Dad on Father's Day with more than the usual tie and bottle of aftershave—host a family brunch in his honor or give him special gifts you've made.

DAD'S DAY BRUNCH

After church, serve Make-Ahead Brunch Casserole, Simple Cinnamon Rolls, and fresh orange juice. For his listening enjoyment, get out the instruments and play a tune while the table is being set.

After the meal, settle him in his favorite chair, feet up and relaxed. Turn on the "Big Game" for him to watch—actually a prerecorded video of the children playing a hearty game of football or a few innings of baseball. Make sure when recording that you break for commercials. Have the commentator (Mom) interview spectators and players, asking them questions about their father such as "What is your favorite thing to do with your dad?" or "Why is your dad the best dad in the world?"

The rest of the day belongs to Dad, who decides if the family will take a walk or a nap, depending on his particular whim! Make sure to give him a copy of the certificate from page 170 featuring Ephesians 6:2–3: "'Honor your father . . .'—which is the first commandment with a promise—'that it may go well with you and that you may enjoy long life on the earth.'" Leave space for each family member to write a comment that honors Dad.

These recipes make a great menu that Dad and your guests will love.

Make-Ahead Brunch Casserole

- 1 pound cooked meat—ground sausage, ham, bacon, or cut-up links
- 10 slices of white bread, cubed (remove crust, if desired)
- 6 large eggs, beaten
- 1½ cups of shredded cheddar cheese
- 1½ cups of milk
- salt and pepper to taste

Cook meat and drain, if necessary. Place bread in the bottom of a greased 9-by-13-inch pan. Place meat on top of the bread. Mix the eggs, milk, cheese, salt, and pepper together and pour over the top of the meat and bread. Use a large spoon or spatula to press down slightly, making sure all the bread has been soaked with the egg mixture.

Cover and refrigerate overnight. In the morning, bake uncovered at 350 degrees until center is set and top is nicely browned, about 35 to 45 minutes.

Simple Cinnamon Rolls

- 2½ teaspoons yeast (one package)
- ¼ cup warm water (110–115 degrees)
- 1 cup whole milk
- ½ cup shortening
- ⅓ cup sugar
- 1 teaspoon salt
- 1 large egg, beaten
- 4 or more cups bread flour
- ⅓ cup brown sugar

- 2 teaspoons ground cinnamon
- 5 tablespoons melted butter

ICING:
- 2 cups powdered sugar
- 2 tablespoons butter, room temperature
- ¾ teaspoon vanilla or orange extract
- milk or cream, as needed

In a small bowl, dissolve yeast in warm water. In a large saucepan, heat milk over high heat until it just begins to boil. Remove from heat. Add shortening, sugar, and salt. Let cool until still slightly warm. Add yeast mixture and egg, and mix well. Add four cups or more bread flour, mixing well, until you have a soft but firm dough. Turn out onto a well-floured counter. Knead for 5 minutes. Place in a well-oiled bowl, cover with a towel, and let rise until doubled, about 1½ hours.

Punch down the dough. On a lightly floured surface, roll into a rectangle about 10 by 14 inches. Brush with melted butter. Mix brown sugar and cinnamon together and sprinkle on top of the dough. Starting with the short side, roll dough and place seam side down on counter. Using a large serrated knife or dental floss, cut into 9 rounds. Place the rolls in a greased 8-inch round cake pan with one roll in the center and the other eight spaced evenly around the sides. Cover again and let rise about 45 minutes to an hour.

Bake at 350 degrees for 15 to 18 minutes. Do not overbake. If the rolls begin to brown too much, cover with a tent of foil. Remove from oven. Cool 5 minutes. Then, using two plates, quickly invert them onto one plate and then again onto the other. Blend icing ingredients together, adding milk only until it is of a thick spreading consistency. Spread over slightly cooled rolls.

Note: the dough may be made in a bread machine using the "dough" setting and adding the ingredients in the order suggested by the machine manufacturer. After the dough cycle is done, proceed from the punching down stage.

LEAVE SECRET MESSAGES

Have members of the family write heartfelt messages to Dad on small strips of paper. These could include memories of special times spent with Dad or things you love about him. Anything goes—just tell him how much he means to you! Then place these warm reminders in a meaningful container. Look for a one-of-a-kind wooden box or beautiful jar, maybe one that includes a motif that is important to Dad. All year long, he can get these out when he is feeling nostalgic and relive significant times with loved ones.

SAY CHEESE

Let your pictures with Dad tell of your love and leave a legacy.

- Take a photo of Dad with each child. Mat and frame each of them in lovely coordinating wooden frames. Hang in a series on the wall for Dad to enjoy.
- Another photo idea begins with snapshots of the kids. Just take pictures of each child highlighting their favorite individual activities. Just as in the preceding idea, mat, frame, and hang in a grouping where family and visitors alike can enjoy!
- Organize a softball or football game for all the dads and kids in the neighborhood. Moms, if you're not in on the game, you could grill out Dad's favorite meats and vegetables or cheer for your special players. Be sure to take a team snapshot.

First Day of Summer

When the longest day of the year arrives on or around June 21, in most places it stays light until well after 10:00 p.m. Start the tradition of holding an annual get-together for family and friends.

Make this a bring-and-share time, varying the menu each year. One time it can be the host providing crock pots of taco meat and the guests contributing the various toppings and both soft and hard shells or shredded lettuce for taco salads.

The next year could be an old-fashioned ice cream social. You provide the ice cream, either store bought or hand cranked during the party. Attendees show up with various toppings—sauces, fruits, nuts, and cherries for the top. Plan some yard games, weather permitting, and end with a bonfire and fixin's for s'mores.

Welcome, summer!

GARDEN PARTY

Sarah smiled. "I had a garden in Maine with dahlias and columbine. And nasturtiums the color of the sun when it sets. I don't know if nasturtiums would grow here."

"Try," said Maggie. "You must have a garden."

Sarah, Plain and Tall by Patricia MacLachlan

When the summer sun begins to shine and the flowers start to open their faces to the warmth of the new season, celebrate the beginning of summer with a garden party. Using the invitations on page 177, ask a few friends and their daughters over for a refreshing, elegant party in the garden that you've labored so hard in. Encourage everyone to wear flowing, floral prints (even hats, if you dare!). Look ahead to the weather to ensure a dry day for the festivities. Then, set up tables in the garden to take full advantage of the beauty, decorate, and enjoy!

- On top of cloth or plastic tablecloths, place moss down the center of the tables for an appropriate backdrop to the rest of your decorations.

- Add gardening gloves, tools, seed packets, or even an old straw hat to the moss.

- Don't forget the fresh cut flowers—straight from your garden. You can place them directly into a beautiful vase or soak florist foam in water, cut to size, and place in various containers. Then cut and poke fresh flowers into the foam. Start with greenery, then the largest flowers, and end with the smaller filler flowers. Use your imagination in choosing the containers—watering cans, birdhouses, chipped terra cotta pots, and even old gardening shoes or boots carry out the theme of your party.

- If you (or a friend) know how to arrange flowers, put on a little demonstration. Have small terra cotta pots and fresh flowers available for each guest. Explain and demonstrate for the ladies how to add flowers and make a centerpiece. Then they can make their own. Walk around and help the ladies with their creations. They'll see how easy it really is.

- Tuck additional watering cans, old boots, and birdhouses here and there around your party area, maybe beside a chair or table or peeking from behind a large plant. You might even try placing a broken pot on its side in the dirt.

- Place a wheelbarrow off to the side with several small pots of lavender or other herbs inside for your guests to take home. Tuck tags with the recipe for Lavender Cookies on page 177 into the pots.

- For a simpler party favor, place packets of seeds inside garden gloves. Don't forget to tuck in Scripture tags (see page 177) featuring Luke 12:27, "Consider how the lilies grow. They do not labor or spin. Yet I tell you, not even Solomon in all his splendor was dressed like one of these." Place these in a gardening basket for your guests to pick up as they leave.

- Keep soft music playing in the background. Try Twila Paris's CD *Perennial*, which features soft, old-fashioned hymns for the seasons of life.

- For the menu, serve a Vegetable Bouquet appetizer, Fruity Chicken Salad on fresh croissants, Chilled Strawberry Soup, tortilla chips with Fresh Garden Salsa (made with peaches—yum!), fresh tossed salad (add fresh, washed nasturtium blossoms for a summery touch), and Lavender Cookies for dessert. Recipes follow.

- Freeze fresh, washed pansy blossoms or mint leaves in ice cubes and place in iced tea or punch.

- A garden party would make a beautiful bridal or baby shower!

Vegetable Bouquet

head of iceberg lettuce	carrot sticks
olives, black and green	toothpicks
chunks of cheddar and Colby-jack cheese	cherry tomatoes
radishes	

Wash vegetables thoroughly. Place lettuce head on a pretty crystal or china plate. Make cuts in the tops of the radishes so that they look like roses. Make cuts lengthwise in the carrot sticks, leaving about 1 inch intact. Place carrot sticks in ice water for two hours to make carrot curls. Place toothpicks in olives, chunks of cheese, tomatoes, radish roses, and carrot curls. Then stick the other end of each toothpick into the head of lettuce to make a beautiful bouquet of vegetables.

Fruity Chicken Salad

4 cups cooked chicken, chopped
2 celery stalks, chopped
$1/2$ cup onion, finely chopped
$1/4$ cup green pepper, chopped
$1/2$ cup dried cherries

$1/2$ cup crushed pineapple, drained
2 tablespoons pineapple juice
4 eggs, hard-boiled, chopped
1 cup salad dressing
1 tablespoon mustard

Mix all ingredients thoroughly. Allow to chill for 4 hours or overnight to combine flavors. Serve on croissants. Makes eight servings.

Chilled Strawberry Soup

2 quarts fresh strawberries
2 cups orange juice
$1/4$ teaspoon ground cinnamon
3 teaspoons quick-cooking tapioca
2 cups buttermilk

1 cup sugar
$1\frac{1}{2}$ tablespoons lemon juice
2 teaspoons grated lemon peel
   fresh mint leaves to garnish

Combine berries, juice, and cinnamon in a blender and process until smooth. You may need to process in two batches. Pour fruit mixture into a large saucepan. Add tapioca and let stand 5 minutes. Over medium-high heat, bring the mixture to a boil. Boil for 2 minutes, stirring constantly. Remove from heat and let cool slightly. Add remaining ingredients and refrigerate for at least two hours. Garnish with fresh mint leaves, if desired. Serves 8–12 people.

Fresh Garden Salsa

3 cups fresh Roma tomatoes, chopped
3 cups fresh, ripe peaches, peeled and chopped
$3/4$ cup diced pineapple, fresh or canned
1 cup red onion, finely chopped

2 jalapeño peppers, seeded and diced
$1/4$ cup lime juice, fresh squeezed
$2/3$ cup fresh cilantro or parsley, chopped (or 3 tablespoons dried)
1 teaspoon or more salt to taste

Chop all needed ingredients, being sure to wear gloves when handling the jalapeño peppers. Combine all ingredients in a bowl. Cover and refrigerate overnight. Serve with tortilla chips or over grilled chicken breasts or mild-flavored fish. Makes 8 cups.

Lavender Cookies

1½	cups flour	½	cup butter
2	teaspoons baking powder	1	cup sugar
½	teaspoon salt	1	teaspoon lavender blossoms

In a small bowl combine flour, baking powder, and salt. Set aside. In a larger bowl, cream together sugar and butter. Add lavender blossoms and stir until well blended. Add in flour mixture and stir until combined. Drop by the teaspoonful onto an ungreased cookie sheet. Bake at 375 degrees for 8 minutes or until lightly browned. Fragrant and delicious.

BICYCLE PARADE

To liven up one of those lazy days of summer and give the neighborhood kids something exciting to do, hold a bicycle parade. Each child decorates his or her bike, tricycle, wagon, or skateboard using a variety of objects.

While streamers were the old standby of the seventies when we were young, today's kids can really get creative when it comes to decorating their parade entry. Balloons, wind socks, shredded metallic paper, and various yarns and ribbon make for great components of a well-decorated bike.

Set a time and meeting place. Have a parade route laid out so that older siblings, parents, and neighbors alike can pull out their lawn chairs and take a seat. Have a boom box blaring tunes from a marching band and let the fun begin.

Afterward, be sure to have some old-fashioned refreshments. Homemade chocolate chip cookies and lemonade are guaranteed to be a hit. You can even award prizes for the most creative or colorful entry. Everyone loves a parade!

A BASKET OF BERRIES

If you live in a region of the country where fruit orchards are at their peak in the late summer months, make a day trip! You'll return not only with some yummy fresh fruit but with some happy memories as well. Many varieties of fruits are at their prime in later summer, including peaches, pears, and raspberries. Strawberries and blueberries tend to come on earlier, usually in June.

Make plans with another family to pack sack lunches, head out for a morning of picking, and then stop at a park to rest and enjoy your lunch. Upon returning home, freeze or make jam out of a portion of that delicious fruit, leaving some for a pie or crisp and for fresh eating too. Here are some of our favorite recipes along with a few fun read-alouds. Happy picking!

Triple Berry Pie

What could be better after a day of berry picking than to enjoy the fruits of your labor between the flaky crusts of a fresh-baked pie? This recipe was a blue-ribbon winner at the 1993 Clinton County Fair in Michigan. Don't forget a scoop of vanilla ice cream on top for the deluxe version.

CRUST:

- 2 cups all-purpose flour
- 1 cup, minus 1 tablespoon butter-flavored shortening
- 1 teaspoon salt
- 1 tablespoon white vinegar
- 5–7 tablespoons ice cold water

FILLING:

Fresh fruit works best, but frozen, thawed, and drained fruit can also be used.

- 1 cup blueberries
- 1 cup raspberries
- 1 cup blackberries
- 1 cup tart red cherries, pitted
- 1 cup sugar
- 3 tablespoons cornstarch
- $\frac{1}{8}$ teaspoon salt
- 2 tablespoons fresh lemon juice
- $\frac{1}{2}$ teaspoon ground nutmeg (optional but delicious!)

Mix flour and salt in a bowl. Cut shortening into flour with a pastry blender or large serving fork until the mixture resembles coarse crumbs. Add cold water and vinegar, stirring to form a soft dough.

Divide the dough in two and roll each out into a circle on a well-floured board. Handle the dough as little as possible so the pastry will be light and flaky. Place one crust in the bottom of a pie pan. Mix filling ingredients in a bowl and place in bottom crust. Lay other crust on top. Crimp and seal edges. Using a fork, poke several times all over the top.

Bake at 350 degrees for 50 to 60 minutes, just until filling begins to bubble and crust is lightly browned. If it begins to brown too quickly, place a tent of foil over the top.

Raspberry-Peach Freezer Jam

- 1½ cups finely chopped fresh, ripe peaches
- 2 cups crushed, fresh raspberries

- 7 cups sugar
- 1 box fruit pectin
- ³/₄ cup water

Bring fruit to room temperature. Measure fruit into a large bowl. Stir in sugar, making sure measuring cups are leveled off with a knife. Measurements must be exact for the jam to set properly. Stir fruit mixture occasionally while preparing pectin.

In a small saucepan, stir pectin into water using a whisk. Bring to a boil over medium-high heat and boil, while stirring, exactly one minute. Stir pectin mixture into fruit mixture. Stir about 3 minutes until sugar is no longer grainy. Pour quickly into plastic freezer containers or pint jars, leaving a half-inch head space at the top. Cover with lids. Let set at room temperature for 24 hours. Store in the refrigerator for up to three weeks or in the freezer for one year.

If you want to share the bounty, give away a couple of pints of this tasty jam. Be sure to attach the tag on page 181 to the rim of the jar with a pretty bow.

Sweet While-You-Wait Memory-Makers

As the pie cools or the jam is setting up, grab one of the following books for an old-fashioned family story time:

- *Blueberries for Sal* by Robert McCloskey. You can almost hear the berries plinking into the pail of a curious little girl named Sal. It is a glorious day to pick blueberries, and this youngster's only problem is that she eats the fat, juicy, blue gems faster than she picks! Robert McCloskey's classic is a wonderful read-aloud during the berry picking season. Join Sal and her mother as they set off in search of blueberries for the winter at the same time as a mother bear and her cub venture out. The story takes an interesting twist as the young ones wander off and by accident end up following the wrong mothers. Delightful!

- *Strawberry Girl* by Lois Lenski. Have you ever wondered what it was like to grow up in the early 1900s? *Strawberry Girl* is about a girl named Birdie Boyer who lived at just that time in American history. She and her family recently moved to the lakes region of Florida. A family with six kids, they are trying to grow strawberries in the harsh conditions of the Florida climate. But trouble is on the horizon. Follow along as the Boyers struggle to get along with their neighbors, the Slaters. Although the going is rough, a happy ending awaits. This is a wonderful book for teaching children about getting along with others. It also offers a peek into a poverty-stricken world many kids today know very little about.

Fourth of July

Celebrate our country's birth with an Independence Day party:

- Let children create a birthday card for our country or perhaps collaborate on a "Happy Birthday, America!" banner to proudly display on the front porch.

- Get out a copy of each of your children's birth certificates. Explain that it includes information about their birth. Then look at a copy of the Declaration of Independence, representing the birth of our country. Have the kids count the number of signatures. Who signed his name the biggest? Do your research and see if you can discover the reason. (Hint: it was so someone in England could read the writing without his spectacles.)

- Read the beautiful words and point out the references to God in some of our great patriotic songs like "America the Beautiful," "The Battle Hymn of the Republic," "The Star-Spangled Banner," and "My Country, 'Tis of Thee."

- Read the book *Fourth of July Story* by Alice Dalgliesh.

- Make a Stars and Stripes Tart (see page 43 for the recipe).

FOR A SWEET, SPARKLIN' TIME

Give your friends a Fourth of July treat they won't forget. Place cans of store-bought blueberry and cherry pie fillings, a jar of marshmallow cream, and some bananas in a red, white, or blue basket. Include a half gallon of vanilla ice cream, a box of sparklers, an ice-cream scoop, and a small American flag. Wish your friends a wonderful Fourth with these makings for Sparkler Sundaes—so they can enjoy the fireworks up close.

FIND THE MEANING BEHIND THE FIREWORKS

You're sure to hear "The Star-Spangled Banner" many times for the Fourth of July holiday—and before any ball game in the summer, for that matter. But does your family know who wrote our national anthem?

Read all about it in the book *By the Dawn's Early Light* by Steven Kroll—a handsome volume illustrated by Dan Andreasen in a way that captures the attention of all ages. Kroll tells how when the War of 1812 raged in America, Francis Scott Key, an important Washington lawyer, penned the words to "The Star-Spangled Banner." With details of the story matching historical reports of the events at Fort McHenry, this book is a perfect patriotic read!

Revel in the Great Outdoors

Experience the scope and scale of this country's beautiful diversity with a camping trip—maybe to the grandeur of the Rocky Mountains, the majesty of the Grand Canyon, or the splendor of Old Faithful geyser at Yellowstone National Park. If those destinations seem out of reach for the calendar or budget, you still can explore the great outdoors at comparatively little cost and go farther for less to experience all God's created. A few pointers as you begin your journey:

- Plan ahead. Most state parks begin taking reservations six months to a year before your expected arrival date—and they fill up. So look at your calendar and get planning.

- Another option is to wait and call a campground the week before you plan to arrive. Often, you can take advantage of someone else's canceled reservations.

- Investigate your state's parks. Most states have a website that will list the different parks and all they have to offer. Our state of Michigan has water and woods, flora and fauna, depending on where you choose to vacation.

- KOA campsites are similar all over the country. They are clean and reasonably priced, and you'll know what to expect wherever you happen to be. Check out their website at www.koa.com for locations across the country and for a handy trip planner.

- Visiting our national parks is a wonderful way to see all the beautiful and varied sights of our country. There are many books available to help you in planning. Try *National Geographic Guide to the National Parks of the United States* by Elizabeth Newhouse. Entrance fees to the various parks vary in price, so be sure to research so you'll know what to expect. Consider a year pass if you'll be visiting more than one park. For a low fee, a Golden Age Passport is available to seniors and is good for their lifetime. For more details, go to www.nps.gov.

FLAG ETIQUETTE

You see Old Glory year round, but did you know there's more to flying that flag right than stringing her up a pole? A quick primer for you and your kids:

The flag should be flown from sunrise to sunset.

Never fly the flag at night without a light to illuminate it.

Whenever raising the flag, do so quickly so that the colors can be unfurled as soon as possible. Lowering the flag should be done slowly with respect and reverence. It should be received by waiting hands and arms.

Do not fly the flag during rain or inclement weather.

After a death or other tragedy, the flag is flown at half staff for thirty days.

The blue background or "union" is displayed at the top and left of the flag.

Never let the flag touch the ground.

Fold your flag properly when storing.

Old flags should be properly disposed of—burned or retired—not just thrown away. Check with your local Boy Scout troop. They will take old, worn flags from you and perform a special ceremony to retire them.

- If you really want to conserve your funds, or you simply want to try camping before heading off into the woods, try setting up a tent right in your own backyard. The kids will think it is great fun, and you will know there is a bathroom nearby!

- Invest in a good quality tent or camper—there's nothing fun about spending the night lying in two inches of fresh rainwater.

- Hope for the best—but prepare for the worst. Take warm clothes for each person even if a heat wave is expected.

- Have rubber "flip-flop" sandals for everyone to wear in the community shower. (You want to bring home great memories, not plantar warts.)

- Put your matches, flashlights, and at least one change of clothing for each family member in plastic bins or large resealable bags.

- Take easy-to-prepare foods, even if they cost a little more. (Remember, you're saving a ton of money just by camping.) Three nights of roasting hot dogs and s'mores over a fire never killed anyone. Where electricity is available, Trish actually takes an electric frying pan and coffeepot to plug into the outlets at campsites. Her family enjoys hamburgers, hot chili, pancakes, and hot coffee on their trips. After preparing the food, you can fill the frying pan with soapy water, heat it up, and do your dishes. Or try a two-burner propane stove; these are easy to transport and use.

- Keep any foods that may possibly melt, like those chocolate bars for the s'mores, in the cooler. If you take crayons to keep the kids busy in the car, keep those in the cooler too. A perfectionist dad doesn't like to see a rainbow of wax on the light-colored upholstery in the backseat of the car. Trust us . . . we know.

- If you want to try cooking in the fire, be sure to take along a cast-iron Dutch oven and some charcoal. Start your fire and heat about twenty pieces of charcoal. When they are hot, try one of the easy favorite recipes we've provided. Everything tastes better cooked over a fire!

- Have a good first-aid kit with you, including items such as bandages, antibiotic ointment, bug repellent, sunblock, sunburn spray, Calamine lotion, upset tummy medication, ipecac syrup (to induce vomiting), a bee-sting kit, and an emergency stash of chocolate (for Mom!).

- Contact the chamber of commerce in each city you will be visiting to see what attractions your family might enjoy. Museums, factory tours, zoos, and parks make great inexpensive side trips (and you get to use a nice clean bathroom for the afternoon).

- The most important tool to take is your sense of humor. Even these "camping-challenged" moms have come to find the fun in roughing it for a few days and seeing their kiddos enjoy the great outdoors.

Easy Chicken and Dumplings

- 2 16-ounce cans of mixed vegetables
- 4 5-ounce cans of chicken
- 2 10½-ounce cans cream of chicken soup
- 2 cups biscuit mix

Open cans of vegetables, then drain liquid into a small bowl and set aside. Place vegetables in Dutch oven. Open cans of chicken and soup and add to oven, stir to combine. Place Dutch oven on a bed of hot coals. Place lid on oven and add ten to twelve hot coals to the top of the lid. With a pair of pliers lift the lid and stir occasionally.

When small bubbles start to form in gravy, start to make dumplings. Add milk or water to liquid from vegetables to make ¾ cup. Add biscuit mix to liquid and stir.

When large bubbles begin to form in gravy, drop teaspoonfuls of dumpling mix onto top of gravy. Replace the top of the oven and the hot coals. Cook for 10 minutes. Stir gently and allow to cook for 5 more minutes.

Apple Cobbler

- 1 29-ounce can of apple pie filling
- 1 box white cake mix
- ½ cup butter or margarine

Line a Dutch oven with aluminum foil and then preheat by placing it on a bed of five or six hot coals, putting the lid on, and positioning eleven to thirteen hot coals on lid. Open can of pie filling. Gently pour filling in the bottom of the oven. Sprinkle dry cake mix over the top. Cut margarine into pats and dot the top of the cake mix. Do not stir.

Place the oven back on the bed of coals and replace lid with charcoal on top. Cook for 1 hour and 15 minutes. Check to see if a knife inserted in the middle comes out clean. If it doesn't, allow to cook for an additional 10 minutes.

Family Reunions

Summertime often finds extended families planning reunions to keep in touch and celebrate their family's heritage. Here are a few ideas to incorporate into your family get-togethers.

WHERE'S THE BEEF?

When it comes to the food planning, recreate some fond and nostalgic memories from your childhood. Have siblings reminisce, listing the foods they most remember from their early years. Then assign the various dishes to family members to make. It doesn't matter if the selections aren't typical picnic fare. What matters is that eating them brings back warm (or funny) memories. Mom's macaroni and cheese, Dad's famous Lipton Onion Soup burgers, Aunt Patty's tried-and-true gelatin salad with mandarin oranges, or Grandma's well-loved Rice Krispies Treats are sure to evoke memories and bring smiles.

For another food idea, have family members bring foods that come from the region in which they now reside. Maybe you have a Floridian who can come with key lime pie, a Texan who contributes three-alarm chili, or a New Englander who whips up a scrumptious seafood salad or Boston baked beans. Although you all originated in the same part of the country, it will be fun to celebrate the diverse places in which you now live with some regional cuisine.

WEAR YOUR GENES ON YOUR SLEEVE

T-shirts are a great idea to identify members of separate families at a large reunion. Just have individual families wear a specific color for the day. You could even tie-dye T-shirts to wear. Or, for a craft to complete on the day of the reunion, have T-shirts ready for monogramming.

Just place T-shirts on a table off to the side, out of the way of the food and main festivities. Then have large stencils ready (one for each beginning letter from the families' last names) along with fabric paint and stencil brushes or sponges. Simply place the stencil on top of the T-shirt and dab with a lightly saturated brush or sponge. Let dry before wearing. What a great souvenir to take home from a special day!

CLAIM YOUR COAT OF ARMS

Back in medieval times when knights wore armor, one of the most important pieces was the shield. Knights used their shields to protect themselves. Each knight put a special design on his shield. In this way knights could be told apart even while their faces were hidden under their helmets. This shield was passed on to each generation.

To carry on this special tradition, have each family design a coat of arms all their own. Supply each family with a poster board cut in the shape of a shield, markers, construction paper, glue, and ribbons. Then let each family design their own coat of arms to represent who they are as a family.

AT OUR HOUSE

A-Camping We Did Go

"Camping!" I exclaimed. "For our first vacation together, you want to go camping? Now that sounds really romantic."

I thought I'd done a thorough job researching my wonderful husband of two months. I knew his strengths and weaknesses, what to expect from his perfectionist temperament; I even knew what brand of toothpaste he insisted on using. But camping? How could I have possibly missed that?

I had so looked forward to marrying into the Ehman clan where vacation stories abounded: viewing Mount Rushmore, touring our nation's capital, sticking toes in the Atlantic—experiences I'd only read about in the pages of a book. I imagined our vacations would include taking in the sights, eating at exquisite out-of-the-way restaurants, and returning to a tastefully decorated, fully functional, modern hotel room to collapse on the comfortable king-sized bed. My idea of roughing it was having slow room service. Now here I stood with the man of my dreams in the midst of a nightmare. He was actually going to expect me to cook over a fire, sleep on the ground, and share a primitive bathroom with hundreds of other "happy campers."

Now I realized that in all my excitement over the stories of grand trips my in-laws and their family had taken, I'd missed one very important fact: they had camped at all of these places . . . and with five children.

Remembering my vows of "for better or for worse" earlier that summer, I swallowed hard and reluctantly agreed to the camping trip. If my dear mother-in-law could do it with five children in tow, then surely I could do it childless.

Todd decided we'd replicate one of his favorite childhood trips east by traveling from our home in southern Michigan to Boston, Massachusetts. Our first stop was a campground in Herkimer, New York, where he'd once hunted for Herkimer "diamonds" by smashing rocks. He chose a campsite right next to the rushing sounds of the river. He loved it. I didn't. I determined that the backseat of our Volkswagen Rabbit was much more comfortable. Once in Boston, we slept on a few square feet of living room floor at the home of one of our bridesmaids. Seemed like a palace to me.

On the return trip, my groom took pity on me and decided we could "bump up" to staying in KOA campground cabins, even though they were ten dollars more a night than a tent site. We returned home, and I vowed to never camp again.

But after three children and many years, I've since eaten my words—many times. I sure hope my dear husband keeps his sense of humor when I insist on a luxury cruise for our twenty-fifth anniversary in five years. With all the money we've saved by a quarter-century of roughing it, I'm sure we'll be able to afford it.

Then I really will be the happiest camper!

Karen

4

CELEBRATE TURNS AND CHANGES: FALL

· · · · · · · · · · · · · · ·

APPLES AND OAK TREES, BACKPACKS AND BLESSINGS

Give thanks to the LORD, for he is good.
His love endures forever.

PSALM 136:1

Bonfires and s'mores; school bells ringing; the smell of apple butter simmering on the stove; a hearty game of touch football in the backyard; a walk in the woods in the crisp autumn air; raking leaves into a huge pile, only to see it come crashing down amidst giggles of glee—so many ways to make memories with family and friends during this favorite time of year! From ways to instill gratitude as you celebrate Thanksgiving traditions to clever ways to serve up the good old apple with a spiritual lesson and a scrumptious recipe, these ideas are sure to please!

Back to School

Marilla was a little worried when she sent Anne off to her first day of school. How would she get along with the other children? Could she possibly keep quiet for an entire day of school?

ANNE OF GREEN GABLES
BY L. M. MONTGOMERY

Looking for ways to make it easier for your kids to hit the books with a smile? Here are some clever ideas to get those pencils flying!

- Every year on the first day of school, take pictures of the kids on the porch, by a special tree in the yard, with their new teacher, or by the door of their school. What a chronicle to display at their high school graduation!

- Make a trip to the store on the eve of the first day of school. While the stores might be busy, it is a great time to get good deals on school supplies. The kids will love picking out new pencils and notebooks. Maybe they'll even be willing to get up the next morning with a little something extra to look forward to.

- Why not "breakfast in bed" on the first day of school? The first time Karen Leif of Saint Johns, Michigan, did this, her kids thought she was crazy! Now it's a tradition that gets the whole family up and at 'em early.

- Pack a special note in your child's lunchbox or write a loving note on the napkin. Karen does this too, and sometimes even includes a picture of the family to help younger students get through the adjustment of being away from home all day.

- Let your child pick out a special "first day of school" outfit.

- Pack their favorite lunch or maybe just some special treats for dessert. Include a few extra for friends.

BACKPACK MINISTRY

During the summer months, children can save up some money by doing extra chores to reach out to a needy family in their church or neighborhood. In early August, your children can shop for some back-to-school supplies, including a small Bible, and fill a backpack for the new school year. Put a handwritten tag on each backpack with the child's name. Drop the backpack on the front porch of the child's house, ring the doorbell, and run. Then sit back and watch the blessings.

Plan a Pumpkin Party

When Kelly's children were preschoolers, they celebrated the harvesttime with a Pumpkin Party. She started this tradition when her oldest son was two, and it has been a fall favorite for over a decade. Soon Kelly's son was old enough to start planning and helping her with the day. What great memories they have of these parties! Here are some things you can do when planning a Pumpkin Party:

- Send out invitations. Everyone, especially children, loves to get fun, personal mail. Be creative and have your children make the invitations. Use pumpkin-patterned paper, blank index cards, or construction paper cut into the shape of pumpkins or leaves.

- Have the children dress up as farmers, scarecrows, and barnyard animals.

- Hold the party outside to enjoy the crisp fall air.

- Serve those fall favorites—fresh donuts and real apple cider.

- For a new twist on an old standby, play "pin the nose on the scarecrow." Draw a large scarecrow face (minus the nose) on a piece of poster board. Then cut out several triangular noses and place some double-sided tape on the back of each one. Blindfold the child and see who can place their nose closest to the center of the scarecrow's face.

- Fill a small kiddie pool with leaves and hide candy, pennies, or stickers in there for a different kind of hide-and-seek game.

- For a fun snack, use string or twine to suspend powdered sugar donuts from a swing set, clothesline, or tree branch. Have children try to eat the donuts without using their hands. See who finishes first—and with the messiest face!

- Bob for apples. Place water in an old washtub or plastic bin. Float apples in the water and see who can pick one up with their teeth.

- While standing above a quart canning jar, try to drop clothespins into it.

- Design an obstacle course. Fill a small wagon with stuffed animals and have children pull the wagon, jump off a bale of straw, roll a small pumpkin to a designated place, and finish by sliding down a slide into a pile of leaves. These are simple things, but preschoolers love them.

- Sing "Old McDonald" and "The Farmer in the Dell"—in rounds, or with different groups chiming in on certain verses or portions of the song.

- Try your hand at face painting: leaves, pumpkins, smiling faces, or footballs.

- Make pinecone bird feeders: spread peanut butter on a large pinecone and roll in birdseed. Hang with string from trees to make a treat for your fine feathered friends.

- Use stickers and markers to decorate simple brown lunch sacks for a special bag to take home all the goodies.

- Before the children go home, take a picture of them all sitting on a bale of straw.

PUMPKIN PRIMERS TO CHECK OUT

For a fun read during the time when the frost is settling on the pumpkin patch, pick up a copy of *The Pumpkin Patch Parable* by Liz Curtis Higgs. This wonderful book tells the tale of a wise farmer who can turn a simple pumpkin into a simply glorious sight. In the same way, God's transforming love can fill each of our hearts with joy and light. Higgs created this parable as a way to share the Good News with her own precious children each harvest season, and it has since become a well-loved fall favorite by children everywhere.

After reading the book, trek off to a pumpkin patch to let your children pick out one of their very own. Return home and wash, cut, clean, and carve just as the wise farmer did to his pumpkins and the way God does to us each day! Then let your lights shine through your newly carved creations for all to see.

Apples Ahoy!

A crisp autumn day can be a perfect time to take a trip to an apple orchard. Return home to whip up a yummy apple creation and read an apple-themed book with the children in your life. Plan a get-together with another family for twice the fun.

APPLES FOR YOUR EYE, YOUR STOMACH— AND STORY TIME

Here are a few favorite books about apples, orchards, and back to the kitchen. Yes, our favorite apple recipes are included.

How Far Would You Go for a Bite?

How to Make an Apple Pie and See the World by Marjorie Priceman. To make an apple pie for the girl in this story requires a trip around the world, as her pantry is stocked with none of the needed components. Fly with her to New England, Europe, and even Sri Lanka to get the needed apples, butter, and cinnamon bark! This delightful fall favorite not only tells a charming story, it sneaks in a geography lesson as well. Included in the back of the book is an apple pie recipe sure to please. Bake it using the fresh-picked fruit from your outing and be thankful you didn't need to travel as far as she to get the same delicious results.

Food for Their Thoughts and Hearts

3 in 1: A Picture of God by Joanne Marchausen. This brightly colored book for toddlers and elementary-aged children uses the apple to teach about God the Father, God the Son, and God the Holy Spirit—the three in one. Small children will begin to understand this biblical truth on a level perfect for them. Our own kids haven't looked at an apple the same since! This book will not only keep their attention but will spark some interesting discussions in the days following.

Keeping-It-Simple Snacks

First of all, to freeze peeled, sliced apples for future use in a crisp or pie, place in a bowl with $1/4$ cup sugar over each 4 cups fruit. Stir gently. Pack into freezer bags or containers. Seal and freeze. Be sure to use a tart cooking apple such as Granny Smith, Spy, or Jonathans. To use, just thaw and drain. Proceed with the recipe as with fresh apples. Use within six months of freezing.

Caramel Apple Dip

- 8 ounces cream cheese
- 1 teaspoon vanilla
- 1/4 cup sugar
- 3/4 cup brown sugar
- 1 cup coarsely chopped salted peanuts

Blend all but peanuts until smooth. Add peanuts just before serving. Use with a tart eating apple such as Granny Smith, Cortland, or Gala. If you must slice the apples long before eating them, soak slices in lemon-lime flavored pop to keep them from turning brown. Drain well and serve with the dip.

Lisa Schroeder of Saint Johns, Michigan, contributed these next two tasty fall treats made with the season's most famous fruit!

Apple Praline Cheesecake

- 1 14-ounce bag of caramels
- 1 1/2 cups graham cracker crumbs
- 3/4 cup sugar, divided
- 1/4 cup butter or margarine, melted
- 1 5-ounce can evaporated milk
- 2 8-ounce packages cream cheese
- 2 eggs
- 1 teaspoon vanilla
- 1 1/2 cups apples, chopped
- 1 tablespoon flour
- 1/2 teaspoon cinnamon
- 3/4 cup pecans (optional)

Preheat oven to 350 degrees. Mix graham cracker crumbs, 1/4 cup sugar, and butter; press onto bottom and 1 inch up sides of a 9-inch springform pan. Unwrap caramels; place in a 2-quart saucepan or microwaveable glass bowl. Add evaporated milk. Melt over low heat, stirring often, until smooth, or cook in microwave on high for 4–5 minutes, stirring every minute and a half.

Reserve 1/2 cup melted caramel mixture. Pour remaining caramel over crust in pan. Sprinkle half of the pecans over caramel, if desired.

Beat cream cheese, remaining 1/2 cup sugar, and vanilla until smooth. Add eggs one at a time, beating smooth after each addition. Toss together 1 cup chopped apple, flour, and cinnamon; fold into cream cheese mixture. Spoon cream cheese mixture over caramel crust. Bake 40 minutes.

Combine reserved caramel mixture and remaining 1/2 cup chopped apple. Spread over cheesecake; sprinkle with remaining pecans. Bake an additional 15 minutes. Loosen cake by running a knife around the edges and let cool before removing from pan. Chill before serving.

Snickers Apple Salad

- 6 Granny Smith apples, cubed but not peeled
- $3/4$ cup cocktail peanuts, chopped, if desired
- 1 8-ounce can crushed pineapple, drained
- 3 king-sized Snickers bars, cut into pieces
- $1/2$ cup butter, softened
- 1 cup powdered sugar
- 1 12-ounce container whipped topping

Put first four ingredients into a large bowl. Mix $1/2$ cup butter and powdered sugar thoroughly. Fold in whipped topping. Pour over apple mixture and gently combine. Delicious!

Caramel Apple Basket

What could be a sweeter fall treat than caramel apples? For a quick yet delicious gift that a neighbor or friend would love, place apples, a bag of caramels, and a bag of craft sticks in a basket. For an extra-special finishing touch, include the gift tag on page 183 featuring Psalm 17:8.

AT OUR HOUSE

Once Upon an Autumn

Every year, I get that old familiar feeling when the first crisp fall day arrives. It's a warm feeling of nostalgia for a simpler, beautiful time when I could smell the burning leaves, feel the wool of my brown and green Tartan plaid skirt itching my legs, and hear the radio faintly cranking out an early 1970s tune. I had the vibrant colors in my box of thirty-two perfectly pointed Crayolas, and my mind teetered between two very crucial topics: who would be my new teacher and what costume would my mom sew for me this year?

It's fall flashback time, and it always makes me wonder if today's children would remember the same happy feelings I had doing simple things like walking among the changing autumn foliage and enjoying natural pleasures like the taste of an apple freshly picked from the tree.

I know we can never exactly replicate the memories we have. Many of today's children are homeschooled or celebrate Harvest Festival instead of Halloween. My family has made some of these same choices. And yet . . .

One year my fall flashback occurred as my three children and I were taking an afternoon stroll in our small Midwestern town. We rounded the corner to the library and were met by the most glorious maple tree that had already turned a bright, golden yellow. The very first tree to change color, it stood out from the others still sporting their summer green. "Mom, look!" Mitchell said. "Ooooohhhh!" baby Spencer cooed. "Can we take home some leaves?" asked Mackenzie.

Before answering, I paused for a moment remembering so vividly my own autumns as a child. I then looked down at my own children, their pockets now stuffed full of leaves, and wondered just what kind of fall memories I'm making for them. "Sure," I said. "Grab a bunch. We'll hang them in the front window."

Back home, with the baby down for a nap, we got out the wax paper and iron and set to work filling our front window with beautiful pressed maple leaves. As we hung each one, I realized there's plenty I can do to help my children see the beauty in God's creation as the seasons change. There are orchards full of fruit waiting to be picked by chubby little hands, hot dogs waiting to be roasted by children with hungry tummies, and precious teens waiting to open up and talk to you as you take an evening stroll.

As that fall turned to winter, I reluctantly took down the golden leaves we'd pressed. I'm determined not to let the memory of that day fade. I've saved our pressed golden leaves.

The next autumn I hung them once again in our picture window just as the mail arrived via our mailman, Mr. Brown. "How beautiful!" he exclaimed. "Takes me back to the time the wife and I pressed leaves with our own kids years ago! Oh, how they loved that!"

I'm not the only dreamer.

Karen

Grandparents Day

In 1978 Congress passed legislation proclaiming the first Sunday after Labor Day as National Grandparents Day. They chose September, the start of autumn, to symbolize the autumn years of life. Whether your tribute is for a first-time grandpa or a grandma of dozens, these ideas will help you to honor, celebrate, and spoil them!

- Have children write a letter to their grandparents telling them what they mean to them. They can share what kinds of things they enjoy about Grandpa and Grandma's house, along with special times they remember sharing with their grandparents. Don't forget to have them draw a picture of themselves with Grandma and Grandpa.

- For an extra-special memento, have grandchildren of any age interview their grandparents. Make out a list of questions ahead of time. Anything goes—whatever the kids might be interested in knowing about Grandma and Grandpa. Maybe it's a simple sketch of their life story, how they met, what the Depression was like, or whether they lived through a war. Then have someone in the family transcribe the interview on their computer. Use a nice font style and maybe some clip art or borders. Distribute to other members of the family for a unique and irreplaceable remembrance!

- Take pictures of all the generations of a family together. Look for chances to take impromptu snapshots—these un-posed photos seem to bring out the personality of the subjects. How about Grandpa and grandson skipping pebbles on a beach or Grandma, mother, and daughter sipping tea? Try taking a photo from behind of Grandpa, father, and son walking along a tree-lined path. The possibilities are endless!

If you know of a grandparent whose grandchildren live far away and are unable to be with them, have your children adopt them on this special day. You could drop by with a yummy treat to share, invite them for dinner, or take in the local attractions together as you teach your children the importance of honoring their elders.

Celebrate the Harvest

If you know anyone who lives on a farm, why not barter sweeping out their barn for using the space for a Farm Harvest Party? To celebrate the wonders of autumn and harvesttime on the farm, invite several families for an afternoon of old-fashioned barnyard games.

Games could include corn husking relays, bag races, and farm trivia. With lots of donuts and cider on hand and a tractor and wagon for a hayride, you have a fabulous fall day planned for friends and family.

To conclude the event, round up everyone for a square dance in the barn or an old-fashioned bonfire complete with all the fixin's for s'mores. If you know of an older local farmer in your church, ask him to come and talk about how farming today compares to what it was like fifty years ago. This can be a rich and memorable day to spend with family and friends. Oh, and don't forget to sweep out the barn again when the party is over!

Skip Halloween for a Hallelujah Night

For an alternative to Halloween, hold a church-wide Hallelujah Night. Children can come dressed as their favorite Bible character or great Christian missionary of old. Or they can get creative when it comes to playing out the Bible theme.

We've seen entire families each with a different fruit costume and—voilà!—the fruit of the Spirit! One youngster tied his Beanie Babies on a rope and let them trail behind him two by two. He was—you guessed it—Noah! The most clever getup: a woman dressed in red flannel pajamas, red socks, and a red stocking cap. On the front, in black, she sported a big letter C. What was she? The Red Sea, of course!

You may wish to have carnival-style games and prizes, a cake or cookie walk, and of course donuts and Hot Spiced Cider (see recipe below) for refreshments. Other ideas:

➤ Hold a pumpkin carving contest. But for a twist, the carving must be based on something from the Bible. How about a candle, based on Psalm 27:1, "The LORD is my light and my salvation—whom shall I fear?" Or what about a cross to symbolize the cross on which Jesus Christ died for us?

❥ Host a "Trunk or Treat" time. In the parking lot of your church, have folks park in a circle with trunks to the inside of the circle. Open your trunks and place your Hallelujah Night candy inside. Have kids travel around the circle saying, "Trunk or Treat!" What a safe, memorable evening you'll have!

Hot Spiced Cider

10 cinnamon sticks, broken up
1 teaspoon whole cloves
2 tablespoons whole allspice
2 quarts apple cider
1 quart water
1 orange, sliced

Mix the first three ingredients in a small bowl. Cut three 7-inch squares of cheesecloth and layer them. Place the spice mixture on top. Gather the four corners and tie with string. Place the spice packet in a large saucepan or slow cooker. Add liquid and orange slices and heat until warm, but do not boil. Serve warm.

Thanksgiving Blessings

How far have we come from what the Pilgrims envisioned for Thanksgiving?

The first Thanksgiving was celebrated by the Pilgrims in December of 1621 to thank God for His provision and protection during their first hard winter in the New World and for His bountiful harvest.

Presidents from George Washington and Abraham Lincoln to Franklin Roosevelt all set aside a day for our nation to pause and be thankful. It was during the Roosevelt administration that the fourth Thursday in November became the official day this holiday was to be observed.

Why let this day be reduced to one for stuffing ourselves silly and watching the big game? The following ideas are designed to help you and your loved ones get back to the basics—the true heart of the holiday as originally intended by the Pilgrims—giving thanks.

READ ALL ABOUT IT

Before all the activity and busyness of Thanksgiving begins, take a moment to curl up with a great book about the meaning behind what can sometimes seem like mayhem if you're hosting the feast. Check out these great reads for the whole family:

Thanksgiving: A Time to Remember by Barbara Rainey. This is a beautiful book telling the story of the Pilgrims' journey to America and their first Thanksgiving in the New World. The story is told from a viewpoint acknowledging God's provision for His people. This story could be read on the days leading up to Thanksgiving or as a special story on Thanksgiving Day. This book offers two stories in one. Reading the larger type only, it's perfect for younger children. If you have older children, read both large and small type for the full story with more details. This wonderful book also includes a CD of beautiful Thanksgiving hymns.

Squanto and the Miracle of Thanksgiving by Eric Metaxas. This great book focuses on Squanto, the Patuxet Indian whose life exhibits the hand of God.

The Thanksgiving Story by Alice Dagliesh is wonderful book written over fifty years ago by a beloved author.

Three Young Pilgrims by Cheryl Harness. When Bartholemew, Remember, and Mary Allerton first arrive on the Mayflower after spending two months at sea, they realize their dream, along with their parents, of coming to Plymouth Colony. What they don't realize is that many in Plymouth won't make it through the first winter, including their own mother. A beautifully detailed, historically accurate, and wonderfully illustrated work—just the pictures have a way of capturing children's attention year after year. Some pages even depict the actual names of the pilgrims, and one page shows a cross section of the Mayflower with its various decks. The book also details the colony's first harvest, made possible only with the help of two friends, Samoset and Squanto. This is a volume you'll pull out year after year. Suitable for all ages.

FIND THE FRUIT OF THE SPIRIT IN A HORN OF PLENTY

> But the fruit of the Spirit is love, joy, peace, patience, kindness, goodness, faithfulness, gentleness and self-control. Against such things there is no law.
>
> GALATIANS 5:22–23

Starting nine days before Thanksgiving, place one piece of fruit in a horn of plenty each day and explain a characteristic of the fruit of the Spirit that we are given by God when we receive Jesus Christ as Savior. Children could give examples of ways Jesus displayed the fruit of the Spirit in His life. For example:

- kiwi for kindness
- lemon for love
- red grapes for gentleness
- Juicy Fruit gum for joy
- fig for faithfulness

- green grapes for goodness
- pear for peace
- strawberry for self-control

Write out Galatians 5:22–23 on a card, or copy the tag provided on page 171, and put it by the horn of plenty. During the nine days, memorize the verse together as a family. Then on Thanksgiving Day recite it together, maybe at your annual Thanksgiving dinner with family. Grandma and Grandpa would love to hear these precious words coming from the mouths of their precious grandchildren!

FILL A BASKET WITH THANK-YOUS

Here's a great project for a Sunday school class or room full of schoolchildren to show how much they appreciate their teacher. Have each child provide one piece of fruit for a gift basket. Then, on a small piece of paper or the tag provided on page 180, have them write down one reason why they thank God for their teacher or leader and attach it to the piece of fruit. Fill the basket with tagged fruit. Each time the teacher eats a piece of fruit, she will be blessed by seeing how she has touched someone's life.

SET THE PLACES WITH SUGAR CONES

Your little ones (and big ones for that matter) can decorate the Thanksgiving table with miniature horns of plenty favors from sugar ice cream cones and fruit-shaped candies. Tie a ribbon around the opening of each sugar cone, then place it on its side on a doily-covered saucer. Fill it with fruit-shaped candies. These could be placed at each plate. Have each child write a verse about thankfulness on a card and decorate. This will surely bless the loved ones seated at the table.

Another idea for place settings is to take a sugar cone and place it, opening down, on a small plate. With small tubes of colored frosting, have the children decorate the cones to look like the teepees the Native Americans resided in. In your nicest hand, write the name of each guest on a piece of paper. Cut out with decorative-edged scissors and prop up beside each teepee. Cute!

RUN THE TABLE WITH THANKS

For a special memory-making heirloom, Trish took a piece of muslin fabric and cut a piece 12 inches wide by 36 inches long. Then she sewed a half-inch hem around all edges. At her family's traditional Thanksgiving get-together, this was placed in the middle of the table with a selection of permanent and fabric markers. Everyone present was then asked to write on the runner something that they were thankful for. Each year as Trish gets this table runner out to display, her family enjoys the old memories and adds some new ones!

REMEMBER THE BLESSINGS

The Sischo family of Ovid, Michigan, has a special way of recalling the blessings they have received throughout the year. Whenever the Lord blesses them in any way, they write that blessing down on a 3-by-5-inch index card and place it in what they call their "blessings basket." They are sure to include any and all gifts given to the family or acts of kindness shown to them during the year. Then on Thanksgiving Day they place the basket on the table along with the turkey and trimmings and take turns reading each card aloud. What a great way to remind ourselves of how the Lord provides for us—just as He promised in His Word that He would.

MAKE A THANKSGIVING TREE

When Tia Houghton of Saint Peters, Missouri, hosted Thanksgiving for her husband's family one year, she came up with a brilliant decoration idea. A few weeks before, she handed out construction-paper leaves to the families that would be attending and asked everyone to take the next few weeks to think about what they were thankful for and write it on a leaf. She then made a tree trunk from grocery bags and simply taped it on the wall.

After everyone arrived on Thanksgiving Day, they spent time taping their leaves to the tree. They actually ended up filling out more leaves to place on the tree as they talked over the blessings and recalled ones they had missed.

Why not keep this holiday decoration up for a while to remind you of all you have to be thankful for?

GIVE THE EXPERIENCE OF WANTING

When Karen's daughter Mackenzie was three years old and no siblings were on the scene, Karen and her husband decided to try to teach a lesson in thankfulness during the Thanksgiving season. They made arrangements with a soup kitchen in a large city a half hour away from their small Midwestern town to help serve Thanksgiving dinner to the homeless.

The morning of the meal, the Ehmans skipped breakfast and went to the shelter to help. Mackenzie was given the task of passing out pickles and olives; her folks let her know that when the serving was over, all of the workers would then be given the leftovers to eat for lunch.

Such a challenge it was for her to cheerfully pass out those pickles and olives—especially the black ones, her favorite! After everyone had been fed and it came time for volunteers to eat, the Ehmans talked with Mackenzie about how hard it was to serve those relishes when she was sooooo hungry herself. They explained that much in the same way, the people they'd just served are in want like this most of their days. The memory has made an indelible difference for Mackenzie, just as it can for your children. Experience can be the best teacher.

At Our House

Faith for the Day—and Then Some

Each year I plan a day filled with Thanksgiving fun for my children. By reading stories, doing crafts, and making food from the first Thanksgiving, we celebrate God's care for the Pilgrims and our thankfulness for all God has blessed us with.

This year I passed the planning on to my eleven-year-old son, who has a love for teaching, organizing, and planning. He carefully thought through our day and thoroughly researched a project for each member of the family. He helped his two-year-old sister make a corncob doll and his two brothers map the Pilgrims' journey to the New World. And then, together, he had us make our own homemade butter—something every family can enjoy.

To make butter, place 1/4 cup heavy whipping cream and a pinch of salt in a baby food jar. Put the lid on and shake the jar until a ball forms. Pour off the resulting buttermilk and place the jar with its ball of butter in the refrigerator until solid.

As we waited for the butter to set, we listened to an audio drama of the story of Squanto. It was a blessing to see my son take over the reins of teaching his siblings and share his love of history with others.

Kelly

WHEN THE GRATEFUL MEET

While the holidays traditionally are a time of laughter and love with family members both immediate and extended, for one group of people in our country they can be a very lonely time. We're speaking of foreign exchange students here studying in the United States.

Most of these students are in our country for three or more years, yet most never see the inside of an American home. Dorms and apartments can be desolate places when most of the other students have gone home for the holidays. Maybe you could include one or more of these people in your family's holiday plans. Contact your local college or university to see if they have a program that matches up students with host families either for a year or a single holiday. Several of our friends have done this on an ongoing basis, and their families have been greatly blessed by it.

When Karen and her family took a Chinese student named Shu to their Ehman family Thanksgiving, the cousins all received a mini crash course in Chinese culture. He also was curious, wanting to know what was stuffed in that bird, what that sauce made out of those bright berries was, and how in the world they could eat that turkey without chopsticks.

As the family dropped off Shu at his dorm that night, they said their good-byes and asked if he had any more questions for them. He shook his head no and then in return asked if the children had anything else to ask him. Four-year-old Mackenzie piped up, "Yes! I have a question. You say your name is Shu. Tell me, do you have a brother named Sock?"

5

CELEBRATE LIGHT
IN THE DARK: WINTER

. . . .

SNOWFLAKES AND CANDY CANES,
HOLIDAYS AND HEARTS

Though your sins are like scarlet, they shall be as white as snow;
though they are red as crimson, they shall be like wool.

ISAIAH 1:18

What if, as a picture painted in *The Chronicles of Narnia* by C. S. Lewis, it were always winter and never Christmas? Or New Year's or Valentine's Day? Winter weather may get you down or keep you inside and restless, but you can make any day extraordinary. And why not celebrate Christmas every day in some way? Claim the hidden joys of winter with these ideas.

First Day of Snow

Celebrate the first day of snow by telling your children just how special they are to the God who made them. Just as God made every snowflake unique and special, He made each of us like no one else. Read them some Bible verses about their uniqueness. Here are a couple of easy activities to illustrate this great truth.

- On a piece of colored construction paper, draw a snowflake using a bottle of white glue. Shake Epsom salt on the glue. Let dry; shake off excess salt. Older children could write Psalm 51:7, "Wash me, and I will be whiter than snow," under the snowflake.

- Catch a falling snowflake. You will need a bowl, a sheet of glass or mirror, cardboard, hairspray, and a magnifying glass. Place the glass and hairspray outside to reach the same temperature as the air. Put the glass on the cardboard and spray it with a thick layer of hairspray. Hold the glass outside until you've caught some snowflakes. Be sure to touch the cardboard, not the glass, so your body heat won't melt the snowflakes. Cover the glass with a bowl to keep away more flakes and leave outside to dry about an hour. You will have preserved the imprints of the flakes to study under a magnifying glass! Do you see two that are the same?

- Bundle up the whole family and head to an elderly person's home to shovel the driveway. Don't forget to take hot cocoa and cookies to share with them afterwards.

- Karen Leif of Saint Johns, Michigan, warms her family's heart with a "Let It Snow" kit. The idea came from a conversation with her mom, who lives in Arizona and misses snow at Christmastime. Karen responded to her mom by sending her a "Let It Snow" kit that you can make too: have children cut out paper snowflakes that can be taped on a window; include a white candle (with a scent name like Winter Wonderland), an old movie like *White Christmas* with Bing Crosby or *Christmas in Connecticut* with Barbara Stanwyk (both have snow themes!), and some Candy Cane Crunch (see the recipe that follows). You could even add a snow globe and watch the flakes fall and a heart warm.

Candy Cane Crunch

24 ounces vanilla or almond bark
2 cups crushed candy canes

Crush the candy canes in a food processor or place the candy canes in a reclosable bag and crush with a rolling pin. Melt the bark in the microwave on high for 2 minutes,

stirring often (or in a pan on the stovetop on low heat). Stir in the crushed candy canes and pour the mixture into a jelly roll pan. Cool the candy. Break it into pieces and place in a cellophane bag; tie shut with a white ribbon. Variation: omit candy canes and add 2 cups slivered almonds or 2 cups red and green candied cherries.

SNOW SWEETS

> Grandma stood by the brass kettle and with the big wooden spoon she poured hot syrup on each plate of snow. It cooled into soft candy, and as fast as it cooled they ate it.
>
> LITTLE HOUSE IN THE BIG WOODS
> BY LAURA INGALLS WILDER

Here are recipes for a sweet treat just like Laura and her sisters would have made in the 1870s back in the big woods of Wisconsin and two other recipes for snowy days.

Maple Snow Candy

Fill a 9-by-13-inch pan with fresh, clean snow. In a medium saucepan, bring 2 cups maple syrup to a slow, steady boil, stirring constantly. When you begin to see granules form in the syrup, take a large spoon or ladle and drizzle syrup onto the snow. Be creative—make various shapes and letters. Allow to cool and harden. Using a slotted spoon, remove hardened candy from snow and enjoy.

Snow Cream

Send the children outside to each collect 4 cups of freshly fallen snow in a bowl. Inside, mix ½ cup milk, 2 tablespoons sugar, and 1 teaspoon vanilla with the snow in each child's bowl. Eat immediately and enjoy your snow cream!

Sweet and Simple Snowballs

   1 12-ounce bag white chocolate chips
½ cup heavy whipping cream
   1 tablespoon butter
½ teaspoon vanilla extract
   1 cup sweetened shredded coconut

Over low heat, melt butter and cream (be careful not to scorch!). Stir in chips and extract until smooth. Cool slightly. Form into 1-inch balls and roll in coconut. Keep in covered container in the refrigerator.

SHARE SOME SOUP

On one of those cold, long days of winter, perk up your spirits by making a steaming pot of vegetable soup. For added fun, before making it, read the classic children's tale *Stone Soup*. This delightful story teaches the truth that if we all share what little we have, the result is something grand! Here is a recipe for Stone Soup for you to try. Serve with a loaf of homemade bread for dipping in the wonderful broth!

Stone Soup

1 large, clean, smooth stone (optional, but kids think it's fun!)
3 tablespoons butter
1 cup diced onion
½ cup sliced celery
1½ cups sliced carrots
½ cup diced green pepper
1 14-ounce can diced tomatoes
3 large potatoes, peeled and cubed

12 cups water
4 bouillon cubes (beef or chicken, depending on the meat you use)
1 teaspoon basil
1 teaspoon garlic powder
½ teaspoon pepper
1½ teaspoons salt
2 cups leftover cooked chicken or beef roast

In a large 6- or 8-quart kettle, sauté onions, celery, carrots, and green pepper in butter for 5 minutes over medium heat. Add tomatoes, potatoes, water, bouillon cubes, spices, and stone if using one. Simmer over medium-low heat for 1 hour. Add meat and simmer half hour longer to blend flavors. Remove stone and serve. Makes 5 quarts of soup.

CURL UP WITH A WINTER'S TALE . . . OR TWO . . .

A snowy day lends itself well to curling up with a good book, some hot cocoa, and the little ones in your life. Here are a few great volumes for exploring on a wintry day. After reading, you may want to make some old-fashioned snowflakes from white paper to hang in your window. Or try your hand at making Sweet and Simple Snowballs from the recipe on page 77. Let it snow!

> ❧ *The Long Winter* by Laura Ingalls Wilder. Gather the family together on those long, chilly winter days to read aloud this wonderful book. Each family member can snuggle up with their favorite blanket or quilt, sip hot cocoa, and discuss the differences between the Ingalls family and yours in coping with winter. Children can even draw pictures about winter then and now while the story is being read. This is a book for all ages, and the time spent together will be memorable.

- *The Snowy Day* by Ezra Jack Keats. This 1963 Caldecott Medal winner is the tale of a lad who wakes up to the wonderful discovery that snow has fallen during the night. He then spends the day in the snow-covered city going on a string of adventures—experimenting with different footprints, making snow angels, knocking snow off of a tree, and trying to make a handmade snowball last until the next day. Keats's illustrations, using cutouts in a collage manner, are sure to be pleasing to your little ones' eyes.

- *The Snowman* by Raymond Briggs. A wonderful, wordless book that depicts the story of a boy and his snowman who comes to life. They spend time exploring each other's worlds, both indoors and outdoors. Appropriate for preschoolers and up, this wintertime classic won the Boston Globe-Horn Book Award and continues to win the hearts of kids every year.

- *Katy and the Big Snow* by Virginia Lee Burton. Katy, a brave and tireless tractor, sports a bulldozer in the summer and a snowplow in the winter. Her hard work makes it possible for the townspeople to do their jobs. Brilliant pictures coupled with plenty of action and attention to detail make this a kids' favorite as they join Katy as she works for the Highway Department of the city of Geoppolis.

- *Snow Family* by Daniel Kirk. This is an enchanting story of a little lad named Jacob who one morning discovers some "snow children"—little snowmen mysteriously come to life—scurrying past his parents' barn. They enjoy a playful time romping through the wintry land, having a snowball fight and even encountering a sleeping bear. Then, however, Jacob realizes that his newfound friends don't have any parents to take care of them. At the urging of some wrens, he builds a mother and father out of snow so their family will be complete. Kirk's brightly colored, whimsical illustrations delight the eye and heart. A perfect wintertime read, even if you dwell in a warm climate!

Keeping Christmas

Christmas was close at hand . . . the season of
hospitality, merriment and openheartedness.

CHARLES DICKENS

With a little time spent planning and preparing along with a few hours one snowy evening, you can reach out to those around you with the love of Christ. It starts with an open heart—and perhaps an open home.

HOLD A CHRISTMAS OPEN HOUSE

Your event need not be fancy, just warm and welcoming so your love will be evident to all that attend. Tips to get you going:

- **Decorate your home with cozy things you already have.** Your Christmas tree with presents underneath (even empty boxes tied with bows) and cute snowmen will do quite nicely.

- **Keep soft music playing** in the background. Instrumental Christmas carols are great because of the mood they set, and your guests can still chit-chat over the music.

- **Provide lots of seating.** Maybe borrow some folding chairs from your church or the neighbor and create cozy seating areas around the Christmas tree or fireplace (if you have one).

- **Tuck in poinsettias around your seating**—or try tall vases filled with holly and evergreens or large boxes wrapped with leftover Christmas wrapping paper.

- **Light many candles** to add a soft, warm glow to the rooms.

- **Provide a small gift for the guests to take home**—one that will remind them of the real meaning of Christmas. Purchase a votive candle for each person who will attend. Then photocopy the triangular design on page 171 onto thick cardstock paper, one copy for each candle. Keeping the printed verse to the inside, fold along the dotted lines, bringing the outside corners together to form a little triangular box. Punch holes in the corners. Place the candle inside and tie the corners together with some pretty ribbon. When the guests open their gift, they will see a reminder of the greatest gift ever given.

- **Keep the menu simple.** Recipes follow for some suggested essentials: Sandwich Roll-Ups, Any-Color Popcorn Balls, Hot Cherry Pie Drink to drink, and Red Velvet Cake for dessert.

Sandwich Roll-Ups

- 8 ounces cream cheese
- 2 tablespoons chopped green onion
- 2 tablespoons sour cream
- 1 tablespoon dried parsley
- 1 teaspoon dried thyme
- 1/4 teaspoon salt
- 1/8 teaspoon pepper
- 1 package 10-inch flour tortillas
- 1/2 pound thinly sliced ham or turkey
- 1/2 pound thinly sliced cheddar or Swiss cheese

Blend cream cheese, green onion, sour cream, and spices together in a small bowl. Spread cream cheese mixture onto tortillas. Layer meat and cheese on top of the herbed cream cheese and roll up tightly. Slice into 1/2-inch rolls and lay flat on a plate or tray for a lovely presentation.

Any-Color Popcorn Balls

- 1 cup light corn syrup
- 1 cup granulated sugar
- 1 4-ounce box flavored gelatin (any flavor will do, but lime and strawberry or cherry are great for Christmas)
- 9 cups popped popcorn

In a small saucepan, combine corn syrup and sugar. Bring just to a boil and remove from heat. Add gelatin and stir until dissolved. In a very large bowl, pour hot mixture over popcorn and stir until well covered. Let stand for a few minutes, then shape into balls. Let cool on wax paper. The kids will love sampling these!

Hot Cherry Pie Drink

- 1 64-ounce container of cranberry juice
- 2 tablespoons of almond extract

  cinnamon sticks

In a slow cooker, combine juice and extract. Heat on low for 2 hours before guests arrive. Serve warm with a cinnamon stick.

Red Velvet Cake

- 2½ cups all-purpose flour
- 1 cup buttermilk
- 1½ cups sugar
- 1½ cups oil
- 1 teaspoon baking soda
- 2 tablespoons cocoa
- 2 ounces red food coloring
- 2 eggs
- 1 teaspoon vanilla
- 1 teaspoon vinegar

FROSTING:

- ½ cup butter
- 16 ounces powdered sugar
- 8 ounces cream cheese
- 1 teaspoon vanilla

For cake, cream together the sugar and oil. Add the eggs and beat well. Stir in vinegar and food coloring until well combined. Sift dry ingredients together. Add flour mixture alternately with but-

INCORPORATE SYMBOLS OF THE SEASON

Evergreens are fragrant symbols of faith and immortality.

Wreaths show God's love never ending like a circle.

Holly, with its sharp green leaves, reminds us of Christ's crown of thorns; the crimson berries remind us of the blood from his brow.

Candles and lights are signs of hope and show us Christ's presence as "the light [that] shines in the darkness" (John 1:5).

Bells and stars beckon us to Christ's birthplace and announce the joy Jesus brings.

Shiny star and angel ornaments remind us of the stars and heavenly host that filled the skies the night Jesus came to Earth, born in a stable.

Pinecones, snowflakes, straw, and herbs remind us of the beauty of nature and the bounty of God's gifts.

Poinsettias were the only gift a small girl in Mexico had to bring the church on Christmas Eve, according to legend. She set her tall, green plant on the altar as her gift to the Christ child. While she prayed, the green leaves changed hue to a brilliant red to represent the love in her heart. The shape of the bloom also represents the Star of Bethlehem.

termilk, beating well each time. Add vanilla and beat well. Bake at 350 degrees in a tube pan for 45 minutes or in two greased and floured cake pans for 25 minutes.

For frosting, cream the butter and cream cheese together. Add vanilla. Sift the sugar and mix together. Spread over cake. Refrigerate cake before serving.

A HAPPY BIRTHDAY TO JESUS!

During the Christmas season, why not celebrate our Savior's birth with a birthday party? What a great idea for the little ones in your life! Here are some ideas to use in preparing a birthday party for the honored guest, Jesus.

- **Send out birthday invitations** on page 176 to those you are inviting. Send early in December, as people tend to get busy this month. Invite family, friends, and neighbors. This can be a way to reach out to those around you who do not know Christ.

- **Encourage children to bring a gift for Jesus, something from their heart for someone most in need.** Ahead of time, find a needy family in your neighborhood, church, or town, and ask each child to bring a gift for a member of that family. Give each child attending a name and age of the person and an idea for a gift (clothes, a toy, or a book). On the day of the party each child brings their wrapped present to be put under the tree. Another idea is to ask children to each bring one item for a needy family's Christmas meal. Make sure you assign this on the invitation or when they RSVP.

- **As each child arrives, give them some playdough** and have them form a figure from the nativity scene.

- **Bake a Red Velvet Cake** (see recipe on page 81) and add decorations and candles to the top.

READ THE CHRISTMAS STORY IN MANY WAYS

Read the story of the first Christmas using a book appropriate for the children attending or a Bible storybook. Using a flannelgraph or a nativity scene will bring the story alive. Other special books to read:

- *One Wintry Night* by Ruth Bell Graham tells the story of God's greatest gift to the world, starting with Adam and Eve.

- *The Crippled Lamb* by Max Lucado. Make a lamb ornament to remind them not only of the lamb Joshua in the story but also that Jesus is the Lamb of God. Cut out a lamb shape from white cardboard. Attach some ribbon or string for hanging. The little ones could glue cotton balls on the lamb, or the older children could wrap white wool yarn around the cardboard.

- *The Christmas Miracle of Jonathan Toomey* by Susan Wojciechowski. Paint a wooden ornament representing figures from the nativity scene.

- *The Legend of the Candy Cane* by Lori Walburg. Demonstrate the symbols of the candy cane, then have each child take home two candy canes along with one of the tags from pages 177 and 180 attached. We have provided one tag describing *The Legend of the Candy Cane* in depth for older children or adults (page 177) and another, simpler version for youngsters (page 180). One candy cane is for them to keep and the other to give away.

- *The Candle in the Window* by Grace Johnson retells a story by Leo Tolstoy, the old legend of how the Christ child walks about on Christmas Eve seeking to enter the hearts of men—and how a candle in the window is what invites Him across the threshold. You can give each child a votive candle as a tangible reminder of the story they've just heard.

AT OUR HOUSE

The Gift of "The Question"

"What are your gold, frankincense, and myrrh this year?" My sister-in-love Renee shared this treasured question with me when we first met in 1988, and it has taken an important role as part of our Christmas celebrations ever since. This symbolic pondering considers:

Gold symbolizes royalty, so what kingly attribute that could only come from God do you see in your life this year?

Frankincense was burned and arose during prayer, so what remembered prayer was answered this year?

Myrrh was a burial spice that accompanied death, so what, by God's mercy, have you "died to" this year?

My then eight-year-old son, Ivan, designed a banner sporting the question, "What are your gold, frankincense, and myrrh this year?" This is now laminated and ready to hang each year as we contemplate the beauty of the newly decorated Christmas tree. As we enjoy a cup of hot chocolate, my husband, Jim, asks "The Question" once again, brand new with this year's circumstances.

The Question is our personal challenge for the month of December, begging us to examine our hearts. On Christmas morning over breakfast, we each in turn answer all three parts of The Question, taking longer with each passing year and trusting heart.

A more dear Christmas gift I can't imagine than to hear each child testify to the work of God in their lives. And it's an important time for them to hear their mom and dad once again recount God's faithfulness.

Debi Davis, Saint Johns, Michigan

CHRISTMAS TALES

"Read it again, Mommy. Pleeeease read it again," begged Mackenzie, my then seven-year-old. Her three-year-old brother, Mitchell, echoed her plea. "Yes, Mommy, especially the part about the little boy and his donkey!"

Their freshly washed faces and still-wet hair glowed in the light of the Christmas tree as they sat with pajamas on next to me on the couch. As a nightly December ritual, they chose a book from our "Baby Jesus Basket" full of storybooks about the birth of Christ. Their favorite this particular year was *The Small One* by Alex Walsh, a fictitious story of a too-small donkey who has to be sold in order to bring in one piece of silver. His young master takes him to town, but no one wants such a small creature except for the village tanner. The donkey is ready to give up his life when a kind man offers to buy him to help carry his pregnant wife to Bethlehem. So the small donkey is given the great task of carrying the mother of Jesus to the stable where He will be born.

I have always loved reading Christmas stories to my children, and each year they receive a new nativity book from my mother. That year, however, my eyes were opened to part of the story that I had been unintentionally leaving out. After tottering over to the basket to put away the book we'd just finished, Mitchell asked me to read him a story from the Bible about the other Jesus.

"What other Jesus?" I asked.

"Not baby Jesus," he replied. "Big Jesus who died on the cross."

Now realizing that he hadn't connected the two in his mind, I sat and explained that the baby Jesus grew up to be the same Jesus who died on the cross to save us from our sins. Somehow he'd figured baby Jesus was a fairy tale and big Jesus was for real.

I realized we adults can do much the same thing. Oh, we know there is just one Jesus and that He is for real, but we are content to leave Him harmlessly in the manger. Somehow a sweet, adorable little baby is acceptable to the world around us. A Lord who calls for men and women to choose either to obey Him or to suffer the consequences is not. But we can't have one part of the story without the other. We must never forget that the hand-hewn manger one day became an old rugged cross. We can't just peer lovingly into the manger without looking obediently to the cross. Baby Jesus deserves our adoration as much as the Lord Jesus deserves our allegiance.

The next year I did not neglect the entire story of the one true Jesus when reading nativity books to our children. Starting with Luke chapter 2 from God's perfect Word before I chose a picture book from our special basket, we read of God's wonderful plan of sending Jesus to earth. We worked on memorizing more of the Scripture in order to put on our annual nativity play for Grandma and Grandpa complete with baby Spencer starring as the Christ child.

Still today we're inventing ways to keep the story going until Easter in order to tie it all together. One woman told me how her family saves their Christmas tree and cuts off all of the branches to leave one large trunk. They then cut off the top about one-third of the way down and use twine to tie the two pieces together in the shape of a cross. They then place the cross in their house where the Christmas tree had been as a visual reminder of the entire life of Christ.

From the cradle to the cross . . . O come, let us adore Him!

Karen

❧ *When Mother Was Eleven-Foot-Four* by Jerry Camery-Hoggatt illustrates how God is the giver of the greatest gift by telling of a mother's love for giving her children extravagant, beautiful, romantic Christmas dreams. When this poor mother runs out of her own Christmas dreams, her children search for the way to be givers of gifts themselves. A nostalgic book with layers of Christian meaning for children and adults.

REEL IN THE HOLIDAYS

The holidays are filled with nostalgic memories of favorite television shows that the three of us remember from growing up. Homework was done quickly after supper because we knew that later that evening, if it was all finished, we could watch *Frosty the Snowman* or *A Charlie Brown Christmas* on network TV. Now that we are all moms ourselves, we have kids with their own tastes in Christmas shows. Here's a list of their favorites:

FOR THE LITTLE ONES:

❧ *The Small One* by Alex Walsh, book and video of the same name. This tale of a too-small donkey that must be sold in order to bring in one piece of silver is a lovely example of the principle from Proverbs that before honor is humility. It is sure to become a well-loved classic.

❧ *The Toy That Saved Christmas* video of VeggieTales fame. This delightfully animated half-hour show from Big Idea Productions cleverly teaches a lesson in contentment while combating the commercialism that often accompanies this time of year. Filled with fun humor even adults will love, it can be a family favorite that is viewed year after year.

FOR THE WHOLE GANG:

❧ *The Christmas Box*, a movie starring Richard Thomas of John Boy fame, will tug at your heartstrings as a workaholic father learns the true meaning of Christmas from an unlikely source. Get out the tissues and get ready to be inspired to make your holidays much less about things and getting and more about people and giving.

❧ *It's a Wonderful Life*, the classic movie starring James Stewart. George Bailey grows up in the small town of Bedford Falls, longing for exciting adventure and foreign travel. However, his lot in life finds him still in his small town, living what he thinks is a small life. Frustrated and haunted by an impending scandal, he decides to end it all on Christmas Eve. Enter a heavenly messenger who shows him a vision: what the world would have been like if George had never been born! All ages will be delighted by the ending to this 1947 movie that was not well received upon its release and won no Oscars but has since become perhaps the best-loved Christmas movie of our time.

❧ *The House without a Christmas Tree*, a video based on the book by Gail Rock. This 1972 movie was a Christmas special on television when we were in grade school. It is a touching story of a heartbroken father who lost his wife suddenly and now sees the image of her in the life of his daughter. He does his best to get rid of anything that reminds him of happiness with his wife, including a relationship with his daughter, Addie. However, she is able to bring love into their home with a Christmas tree that she desperately wants. As a result she brings love to her father's heart as well. A very powerful story of the true meaning of Christmas.

EIGHT WAYS TO MAKE CHRISTMAS BRIGHTER

> They were all so happy they could hardly speak at first. They just looked with shining eyes at those lovely Christmas presents. But Laura was happiest of all. Laura had a rag doll.
>
> *LITTLE HOUSE IN THE BIG WOODS*
> BY LAURA INGALLS WILDER

The best Christmas will cost you something—but more than money. The best Christmas will cost you some time, creativity, and love. These ideas show you how to spend yourself—but not necessarily your budget.

1. Making the Nativity Real and Remembered

The nativity scene and story of Jesus's birth may be the most dramatized, reenacted, painted, composed about, and otherwise depicted event in history. But how can you write the story on your loved ones' hearts, not just plant it in their heads? These ideas help, and the moments experienced with the nativity can be living memories.

Tell the story over and over. For a keepsake to treasure in years to come, record your children each year telling the nativity story into a tape recorder. Toddlers will be able to articulate just the basics about the Christ child, the manger, the angels, and the shepherds. As they grow, more details will be added to their narration. Once they are old enough to read, let them read the story from Luke 2 out loud to be recorded. It will be fun to hear how their voices change from year to year. A great present to give grandparents!

Give the nativity. When your children are young, purchase nativity sets for each of them to have when they are grown and leave your home. Figure out how many pieces are in the set. Then each year give them one piece in their stocking, timing it so that they get the last piece the year they are eighteen.

Live the nativity. Take in a living nativity experience. Many churches reenact the first Christmas by having church members dress up as the characters found in Luke chapter 2. Children especially love to drive by and see the holy family, angels, shepherds, and wise men. Return home for some hot spiced cider (the recipe's on page 68).

Go on a hunt for Jesus. Hide a baby boy doll, and on Christmas morning crank up a yuletide tune to awaken the kids. Then hunt for baby Jesus, like the wise men of old. After He's placed in a makeshift manger, read the Christmas story from Luke 2 before opening your presents.

Build suspense along with the story. Place your nativity set out piece by piece, telling the Christmas story as it is found in Scripture. The first night, place Mary out all alone as you read the part of the Bible where she is first mentioned. The next night comes the angel who appears to her. The following night Joseph appears, and so on. You'll soon be placing the animals, shepherds, baby Jesus, and finally the wise men, who arrived a few years after Christ was born. This is a great way to make the Christmas story last over several days, and the kids will look forward to the new character put out each night.

2. Living by the Light

For a fun activity that sneaks in a lesson, have one evening where you use no lights but do everything by candlelight. Eat by candlelight. Wash the dishes by candlelight. Get ready for bed by candlelight. (This is getting tricky!) Set the family on the couch and read (by candlelight, of course) 1 John 1:5, "God is light; in him there is no darkness at all." Talk about this verse and what our lives would be like if we had no lights. Talk also about what our lives would be like if we didn't have the light of Christ. Then hop in the car and go look at your town's Christmas lights.

Many cultures place a candle in the window from dusk to dawn on Christmas Eve, signifying the star that guided the wise men to Jesus. For fire safety reasons, we suggest using an electric candle.

3. Trekking for a Tree

For a unique family outing after Christmas, take a tree trek. Get ahold of a copy of the wonderfully illustrated book *The Night Tree* by Eve Bunting. It tells of a family's annual outing to decorate a tree in the forest with popcorn strings, fruits, and other treasures that the animals will

One Way Your Experience Can Shape Your Holiday

"For Us, It's All about the Eve"

We don't celebrate Christmas in the way most people do—no waking up early Christmas morning to dive into the presents under the tree for us. Instead, we actually celebrate Christmas on Christmas Eve.

We begin with a special dinner in the late afternoon and go all-out with all kinds of wonderful recipes. Through the years entrees have included Succulent Beef Tenderloin and Herbed Cornish Hens. Favorite side dishes are Twice Baked Potatoes and, of course, the old, faithful Green Bean Casserole. After this lovely dinner we open our stockings before heading off to our church's Christmas Eve candlelight service, complete with a candlelight singing of "Silent Night." Then it's back home to exchange the rest of our presents.

Our son doesn't seem any the worse for this unusual version of Christmas; he doesn't seem embarrassed when his friends question him about what he received on Christmas morning. He actually seems slightly proud to explain, "We get to open our presents on Christmas Eve!"

Our tradition is our own—based on the fact that my husband asked me to marry him on Christmas Eve. What better time to celebrate both the birth of our Savior and the beginning of our family?

Trish

be delighted to find and eat. After reading the book, your family can trek out to the woods to decorate your own night tree. Then return home for a round of hot cocoa, just like the family in the story.

4. Being a Card

Maria Witte of Normal, Illinois, describes a great family tradition: "One of my warmest memories is of my mom decorating the house for Christmas with the many Christmas cards she was receiving. She would tape them around the large entryway to our living room. I remember how festive it felt! Plus it gave my mom (and our family) a creative way to continue enjoying the cards. I have carried on this simple tradition in my own home (around our large kitchen doorway) at Christmastime and when new babies have joined our family. It provides some sweet decorating and a reminder of how many people love us!"

Take those Christmas cards you receive and make collage placemats. Just take a few cards and place them together, shifting and exchanging cards until you are pleased with the arrangement, which can be any size or shape desired. Then cut two pieces of clear adhesive-backed paper larger than your card collage. Peel off the backing of one piece and place your arrangement of cards on top. Now peel the backing off the other piece and carefully place on top. Rub with your fingers to assure a good hold, and trim around the edge. You'll have not only a beautiful table but a warm reminder of friends and family as well.

5. Making a Manger for the Morning

Renee Schafer of DeWitt, Michigan, says, "We place a special manger scene in front of the fireplace on Christmas morning—before any breakfast or gifts. The children turn on the light that illuminates the area surrounding the baby in the manger. Then they lay on their tummies and look into the manger while Dad reads the Christmas story from Luke chapter 2. Until this tradition is completed, the children don't look to the gifts or even the filling of their tummies. The focus is on God's precious gift to us and our thankfulness and praise to Him. It is a very meaningful bonding time we share as a family."

6. Keeping a Silent Night

Before the hustle of Christmas presents distracts her family, Cheryl Pacilio of Bloomington, Illinois, uses the peaceful time after the Christmas Eve church service to remind her family how much they really value each other. During the previous days or weeks, each family member takes the time to write a personal note or letter (or draw a picture, depending upon the skills of the author) to every other family member. They use their Christmas stockings as "mailboxes." After starting a fire they sit quietly reading and weeping over the tender sentiments shared. Some years they have also shared the homemade gifts that the kids have made so that they get their proper appreciation before the hubbub of Santa.

To top off Christmas Eve, Cheryl says her family turns in sleepover style—all four kids (whose ages span eleven years) plus Mom and Dad in one bedroom.

The Pacilios establish an agreed-upon wake-up time, and Cheryl says: "That, in itself, is a result of the tender attitude each takes to bed. It's a tradition they made up themselves!"

7. Searching for the Gift of Christ

Jayne Harris of DeWitt, Michigan, says her children search among the angels on her tree (which always hosts an angel theme) for five hidden letter ornaments that spell out JESUS. "The kids must find these letters in the tree before opening any presents," she says, "and this keeps God's gift from being forgotten."

8. The Three Gifts

Karen's family has the tradition of giving their children just three gifts, in addition to their stocking stuffers, on Christmas morning. This is an attempt to simplify and teach a lesson on contentment. They remind their children that the Christ child received three gifts—gold, frankincense, and myrrh—and so each year, that is the same number they will receive. Each Christmas they open one gift to wear, one item to read, and one thing to play with.

Colleen Redfield of Rochester, Minnesota, adds a new twist on this idea. "Our children receive gifts on Christmas morning that mirror the same gifts that were given to Jesus by the Magi. We've adapted them a bit, but the result has been a wonderful way to remember those first gifts given so long ago.

"First they receive a 'gold' gift. This symbolizes the gold Jesus received. It's precious and worth a lot. The gold gift for our child is the one big gift they may want, something that is their heart's desire.

"Next is their 'frankincense' gift. This was an incense or spice used in Jesus's time in the temple, something that was used during prayer and fasting. A frankincense gift should be a gift that will draw them closer to God. This can be a new Bible, a Christian book or video, or for the young ones, a play nativity or Noah's ark set.

"Finally is their 'myrrh' gift. This was the fluid that was used upon death, covering the entire body. Today, it could be translated into something that they need that covers the body—pajamas, a new coat, a sweater, or pants."

What a great way to teach children a lesson in Bible history!

BEYOND THE MALL: THE GIFTS OF CHRISTMAS

Brightly wrapped gifts and perfect presents may be the only part of Christmas that your friends and even family remember. But it doesn't have to be that way. Gifts can evoke memories and plant seeds of love, faith, and hope.

Make the Gifts a Family and Friendly Affair

Trish loves to make handmade gifts for Christmas—and not just in the fall but year round. In fact, she's found strength in numbers by getting together with friends who feel this same way; they plan an evening of crafting for the holidays.

They start a couple of weeks ahead of the planned evening by shopping for the needed supplies to make a project or two. Then one friend prepares a simple meal of soup and bread and another brings a special dessert.

After a relaxed meal, the friends dig into their project. They divide the jobs and go into high-production mode, each person cutting or gluing and completing the crafts in assembly-line style.

"Not only do we get a great start to our holiday projects," Trish says, "but we're storing up memories to get out later and savor over a hot cup of coffee!"

Find the Unusual—to Give and Receive

Kelly Hughes of Bloomington, Illinois, says some of the best memories in her family come from traditional gifts—both gifts received and those given:

> ❧ "When my brother was living in San Francisco, he bought my kids some frankincense and myrrh from an Indian grocery. Every Christmas since, we've brought out these precious

gifts, along with some 'gold' jewelry, to talk about the wise men's choices and meaning in each of their offerings to Christ Jesus." Read more in "The Question" on page 83.

- "We place an empty 'manger' in our home. My dad actually built us a manger, but you could use a bowl, box, or basket. Every time one of the kids performs a kind act for another family member, they get to put some straw in the manger. On Christmas Eve, we place a special baby Jesus there and marvel at experiencing firsthand his arrival. (The 'baby' is actually a doll I pack away and use only for this.) Our goal is for baby Jesus to have plenty of hay for his head."

- "For a great stocking stuffer, create a coupon book of gifts—kind favors you will do throughout the year."

- "Laminate Christmas pictures your kids have drawn to use as their placemats."

- "My mom buys the kids pj's every Christmas and has them washed and ready to wear before she wraps them. This way the kids can wear them to bed on Christmas Eve. They are covered in love this way and kept warm in spirit too."

- "We buy a new book for each of our children every year. This way the kids have a library to take (sniff) when they leave home. We do the same thing with ornaments for the tree—each child gets something 'new' (at least to us) every year, so they will have a full tree when they get out on their own."

- "At dinner during the Christmas season, we pray for each of the families we have received cards from that day."

- "Right after Thanksgiving we buy our family a present of a holiday puzzle—at least 1,000 pieces—that we immediately set out to try to finish before Christmas. This encourages time together as a family."

- "For younger kids, place hot chocolate in sipper cups with lids to take in the car on the annual Christmas lights tour around town."

WHEN HOLIDAYS REMIND YOU OF HURTS

When Trish's sister Cindy suddenly found herself a single mother of two young children, she found it difficult to think of ever celebrating holidays and birthdays in the same way. She realized, however, that her children needed (and looked forward to) the rituals and traditions of holidays and the hope and possibilities of special days. She decided to take her cues from them.

Although it was too painful to relive long-held traditions, she decided to embark on a new phase of their lives—with their own new traditions. So instead of Thanksgiving at Grandma's, they got together with two other families that were special to them. That day was so successful that they think they will do this every year.

At Christmastime, the small family went shopping for a new Christmas tree and ornaments. The day after Thanksgiving, they worked together to put up the new tree, and all of them set to work decorating it (a task that had previously fallen to Cindy alone).

When completed, they had a beautiful tree they could all be proud of, full of their new ornaments as well as some homemade masterpieces they had crafted that day—with most of the ornaments hung at the children's eye level, about four feet off the ground.

Perhaps you too have experienced some hurt or tragedy in the recent past. If you find it too painful to try to recreate celebrations as they once were, try designing some new ones of your very own. As we look forward to holidays and spending time with those we love, these new traditions can actually bring a bit of healing to hurting hearts.

🍂 "Early on we invested in a plastic nativity set that the kids can interact with so they can marvel at the way Christ came to us from heaven—as a baby, in a manger, to poor parents."

REMEMBER OL' SAINT NICK

The legend of Saint Nicholas has become so real to Karen's family—and helps us live out our Christian faith—that they've made a tradition of celebrating Saint Nicholas Day.

First, about the legend: Saint Nicholas was a real person who lived from 270 to 310 and was known for his great generosity and desire to remain anonymous. He lived in Myra, a town in Asia Minor, which is modern day Turkey. Once the bishop of Myra, he made rounds under the cover of night to bring gifts to the poor and children. He died on December 6, so December 5 is now known as Saint Nicholas's Eve.

Various European immigrants brought their own well-loved St. Nicholas holiday traditions to the United States; over time, these have blended into celebrations like one the Ehmans' friend Marielle, a native of Switzerland, has passed along.

The celebration: Marielle tells that as a child she would leave one of her boots out on December 5. In the morning, the boot would be filled with fruits, nuts, and a few trinkets.

Now the Ehmans and their circle of friends select one of the fathers to act as Saint Nicholas, while the moms mix fruits, nuts, and trinkets in large, reclosable bags labeled with each child's name and a description of their boot. (No boot mix-ups!) The father who portrays Saint Nick brings the gifts under cover of night or on his way to work in the wee hours of the morning.

Just as the real Saint Nick wanted to remain anonymous, the children aren't told which father plays Saint Nick each year—they have to wait until the following year for the secret to be revealed. Then on that day each family chooses something good to do for the less fortunate: deliver a fruit basket to a shut-in from church or new toys to the children's ward at the local hospital. The goal, Karen says, is to carry on the spirit of giving that Saint Nicholas started all those years ago.

SIMPLIFY YOUR HOPES AND DREAMS

We all know how frazzled and busy the holiday season can become, but these tips can streamline the celebrations for a joyous time—and just maybe a few silent nights.

🍂 **Reevaluate your holidays with an eye on hopes, dreams, and expectations.** What are your family's favorite traditions? What can you cut out of your schedule that will not affect these traditions? What is your least favorite holiday duty? Does this really need to be done? Or how can it be changed to make it more enjoyable? How can other family members pitch in so less work falls on Mom's shoulders?

- **Organize! List what you need to get—and get done—this season.** Now create a schedule for doing these things, stick to your decisions, and start another list of things you need to purchase to complete your holiday tasks.

BEYOND CHRISTMAS

You can do so much on the fly, year round, for Christmas that will make each season's celebration fall into place more easily so you can spend time on people, not projects! The best tips:

- Right after Christmas, look for holiday items at clearance prices. Cards, decorations, wrapping paper, and supplies can be found at half price or less. Keep these things in a clearly labeled box or plastic tub, and throughout the year toss in your sale items. You may not need to spend a dime more come next fall!

- Keep a notebook in a handy place to list Christmas gift ideas for particular people and shop throughout the year. This eases the strain on the family budget come December and allows you to find better deals and finish your shopping early too. Just be sure to keep the gifts in one location—maybe add to your notebook a list of what's been purchased and where it's stored so there are no gifts gone MIA (missing in action)!

- Develop holiday ideas throughout the year. When you see a recipe you'd like to try or a decorating notion that would be perfect for your home, note it, store it, or clip a copy and put it in your Christmas notebook. Look! Everything's at your fingertips for next year's celebration!

Welcome the New Year!

This year, skip the New Year's Eve party scene and have a family celebration. If your children are little, start the party early, before their bedtime, or put them to bed early and then wake them up at 10:00 p.m. for the party.

Build a fire in the fireplace, if you have one, and serve some special snacks. Snacks that are a tradition each year are always a hit. Get out some games that everyone can enjoy. You may even want to pick up some clearance items from the after-Christmas sales and wrap them for prizes for the games.

As the year draws to a close, have each family member draw a picture of or write about a low and a high point of his or her year. Go around the room and have each family member share. This will provide many laughs as well as tears as you close out the year.

Right before the stroke of midnight, fall on your knees as a family and pray in the New Year. You could pray for our country and its leaders, a closer walk with the Lord, and a deeper commitment to each other as a family. This night can be a precious time to cherish, and many memories will be built that last a lifetime.

AS THE BALL DROPS

The Jim and Debi Davis family of Saint Johns, Michigan, has a couple of New Year's traditions that have become much-anticipated events in the life of their entire family.

When the children were very young, Jim and Debi decided to turn down all New Year's Eve invitations and make it a fun and meaningful night for their family. A Family New Year's Welcoming quickly became a tradition, and it is a pivotal time to come together in prayer and thanksgiving before the coming year.

With their favorite array of appetizers and games ready, the Davis family begins the evening with a game their oldest child invented. They fondly call it "Pictionary—Davis Style." Everyone sits around the table with a pad and pencil, the timer is set, and each person quickly draws a memorable event of the year. The real challenge comes next when everyone gets to guess what that event is!

More games follow, ending around 11:30 p.m. when the family gathers to sing praises to God, culminating with prayer for the coming year at midnight. The younger children's favorite part of the night comes last—smashing a piñata to welcome in the new year.

As the new year brings its own challenges, Debi says they often think back to that time of family prayer and take confidence once again in God's provision, direction, and care.

A FAMILY HERITAGE DINNER

Food has a way of creating memories, and the Davis family could write a book on how. Their Family Heritage Dinner on New Year's Day has won an important place on their calendar and in their hearts. It's a meal that provides a great foundation for the coming year, and yummy recipes too: Creamed Potatoes, Soupy BBQ Chicken, and Righteous Apple Pie (yes, Debi's grandmother really did call her apple pie "righteous"!).

Here's how Family Heritage Dinner works: on New Year's Day, Debi does her best to recreate one recipe from each mother and grandmother. This took a little researching with her husband's family, Debi says, "but once found, these cherished recipes will never leave my kitchen!"

Over dinner, she and husband Jim take turns telling stories about each mother and grandmother and how they remember them serving the dishes gracing the table.

"It's the same strange menu every year, along with many of the same stories that will now go down through the generations," Debi says.

As for the centerpiece and visuals that go along with the stories, Debi sets out small, framed photos of each of their mothers and grandmothers. "What a treat to have the grandparents join in the meal when they're available—it's almost like they're telling these stories firsthand!"

Grandma Lucy's Creamed Potatoes, 1933

- 1 large white onion, chopped
- 1 stick butter
- 5 lbs. white potatoes, peeled and diced
- 3 cups water
- 1/2 cup flour
- 2 cups milk
- salt and pepper to taste

Sauté onions in butter until transparent. Add potatoes and water, cook until potatoes are tender. Wire whisk the flour into the milk, add to potatoes, and heat until thickened. Add salt and pepper to taste. Potatoes should be thick enough to serve on a dinner plate.

Grandma Elsie Belle's Righteous Apple Pie, 1947

CRUST:
- 1 1/2 cups all-purpose flour
- 1/4 teaspoon salt
- 3/4 cup shortening
- 3 tablespoons cream or whole milk, well chilled
- 1 beaten egg
- 1/2 teaspoon vinegar

FILLING:
- 1/2 cup white sugar
- 3/4 teaspoon cinnamon
- 1/8 teaspoon salt
- 6 cups thinly sliced Spy apples

TOPPING:
- 3/4 cups firmly packed brown sugar
- 3/4 cup all-purpose flour
- 1/3 cup butter

Mix flour and salt from list of crust ingredients. Cut in shortening. Mix remaining crust ingredients and add to the flour mixture. Stir lightly until a ball forms. Wrap in plastic wrap and chill two hours. Remove from refrigerator. Preheat oven to 400 degrees. Roll crust out on lightly floured surface, making a circle slightly larger than a 9- or 10-inch pie pan. Place crust in pan and crimp the edges. Mix filling ingredients in a medium bowl and transfer to crust. Mix all topping ingredients until crumbly. Sprinkle over apples. Bake at 400 degrees for 35–40 minutes until apples are tender. Grandma always served this with a large slice of cheddar cheese on the side!

Grandma Isabelle's Stovetop BBQ Chicken, 1954

1 large chicken, plucked and pan ready (*cut up)
1 cup regular (*white) vinegar
2 cups brown sugar
2 cups catsup
   just enough water to cover chicken

Cook chicken and all ingredients in large pot, covered, for at least 3 hours, until dinner time. Serve juice in a gravy boat, good over potatoes. If juice is not thick enough, stir ½ cup flour into 1 cup cold water, add to juice and cook, stirring constantly until thickened.

*2004 notes

Valentine's Day

And now these three remain: faith, hope and love.
But the greatest of these is love.

1 CORINTHIANS 13:13

As the world is focused on candy hearts and flowers, valentines and chocolate, now is the perfect time for us to emphasize the true meaning of love—the sacrificial, selfless love of our Savior. Whether you're participating in a Victorian tea or simply celebrating within your own home, seek to model Christ's love to those around you as you try out some of the following ideas.

VICTORIAN TEA PARTY

Go back in time, don your frilly dresses, and enjoy a time of complete elegance for a Valentine's Day Victorian Tea Party. You can plan a very simple tea, inviting close friends to celebrate the love you share in Christ. What a great time you and your daughter will have planning the menu that will be served and enjoying the time spent together preparing the food. There are many books on tea parties available to help with ideas, but here are a few to get you started. And remember, simple is best!

- Use tea bags to make clever homemade invitations for your guests. Simply remove the tags from the strings of the tea bags. Replace with the small invitation tag from page 181. Just photocopy enough for your guests and attach to the strings of the tea bags.
- Set an old-fashioned table with a lace tablecloth or use doilies (paper or cloth) as placemats.

- Use your best china or have those you have invited bring their own place settings.

- If you have little ones, use a miniature tea set or purchase some small plastic tea cups (children could also take these cups home).

- Add a vase of fresh flowers as a centerpiece.

- To enhance the atmosphere, play some beautiful harp or piano music.

- Choose several kinds of brewed tea to serve to your guests. Davidson's Tea has a tea especially for children—very fruity and sweet, and free of caffeine.

- Serve some light refreshments with your tea, such as tiny muffins; scones with some jams, jellies, or cream cheese; fruit; vegetables; or cakes.

- Plan a short devotional from 1 Corinthians 13.

- Recite a poem about God's love.

- Read some verses on the love of Christ from the Bible.

- Lead a prayer blessing the mothers and daughters in attendance.

- Research and tell about the history of tea.

- Give those attending a special remembrance of the tea, such as a book, a bookmark handmade with dried flowers with a love verse written on it, or a special tea bag.

TALK ABOUT LOVE

Read the "love chapter" of the Bible, 1 Corinthians 13, aloud as a family. Talk about the characteristics of love and how you as a family can display them to each other in the days ahead.

Then hang a copy of the certificate from page 172 on your refrigerator or in another prominent place. On this certificate the verses are given, but each time the word *love* should appear, a blank is left instead. Whenever one of you catches someone else in the family exhibiting that particular characteristic, write that person's name in the blank. On Valentine's Day, remove the certificate and read it out loud. The result will be something like this: "Hannah is patient. Matthew is kind. Dad does not envy . . ."

Make it your family's goal to exhibit those qualities all through the year!

WRITE IT ON THEIR HEARTS

A few days before Valentine's Day, Kelly Hughes of Bloomington, Illinois, takes each member of the family aside and asks them to explain what they love about the other people in the family.

She writes these things on paper hearts and strings the hearts together to make a streamer for each family member.

The night before Valentine's Day, the streamers are hung on each member of the family's door so they can awaken to a surprise curtain of loving words.

The love chains then lead to a pancake breakfast on Valentine's morning—not just any pancakes, though! Red food coloring is added to the pancake batter, and a huge metal cookie cutter is used to make heart-shaped pancakes. Just set the cutter on your frying pan or griddle, then fill it with batter. When one side is done, remove the cutter with tongs (you'll burn your fingers if you try to do this by hand!).

SEE RED!

Celebrate in true Valentine's Day form with a family Red Dinner. Let the children be creative and decorate the table with homemade valentines and hearts. Cover the table with a red cloth and purchase some fun valentine plates, cups, and napkins, or simply use all red. Use large rectangular paper doilies as placemats under the plates. Choose a menu that consists of anything red or containing hearts. Here are some ideas to get your creative juices flowing:

- lasagna or spaghetti
- red finger gelatin cut in the shape of hearts
- lettuce salad with tomatoes and French dressing
- applesauce with red food coloring added
- red punch, pop, or juice
- Red Velvet Cake (see page 81) or your favorite red dessert
- red peppers with ranch dip (for serving, you could even place the dip inside a red pepper that's been cleaned out)
- biscuits cut in the shape of hearts with strawberry jam
- chocolate—we know this isn't a "red" recipe, but what would Valentine's Day be without it?

AT OUR HOUSE

Keeping the Love Jar Filled

For the month of February, we keep a jar on our kitchen table and invite everyone to drop in love notes for one another throughout the month. When one person appreciates something that another family member has done for them or just something they love about that person, they write it down and drop it into the jar. At the end of the month, everyone gets to pull out their notes and read these love letters.

Shawna Shaw, Grand Ledge, Michigan

Hot Fudge Ice Cream Cake

Here's a deliciously decadent Valentine's Day dessert. Be sure to top with a scoop of vanilla ice cream. Yum!

1	cup all-purpose flour	1/4	cup vegetable oil
3/4	cup sugar	1	teaspoon vanilla extract
2	tablespoons unsweetened cocoa	1	cup firmly packed brown sugar
1 1/2	teaspoons baking powder	1/4	cup unsweetened cocoa
1/4	teaspoon salt	1 3/4	cups boiling water
1/2	cup milk		

Combine first five ingredients and place in an ungreased 9-inch square pan. Add milk and vanilla, stirring until smooth with a rubber spatula. Combine brown sugar and ¼ cup of the cocoa. Sprinkle over the batter and then pour the water over the batter, but do not stir. Bake at 350 degrees for 40 minutes. The cake will rise to the top and a layer of ooey-gooey fudge will settle on the bottom. Serve warm with whipped cream or ice cream. Makes 6 servings.

Black History Month

Our nation traditionally honors African Americans during the month of February. With our country's history of slavery, the Civil War, and the struggle since for racial equality, it is important no matter what your race to pause at his time of year and reflect. It is especially important to model this for our children. Here are some ideas to try:

SOME ACTION/INTERACTION FOR RECONCILIATION

Many of us in our nation still live in a town or area that is not racially diverse. Use this time to break that trend, at least for a little while. With your family or friends, visit an ethnic restaurant, take in a local African American art exhibit, or head out to a black history museum.

If you are not part of a minority ethnic group, now is a good time to take your children to a church where they will not only be visitors but will have skin color different from the majority of those in attendance. Upon arrival home, discuss the experience and strive to promote understanding of those different from them, pointing out the fact that "Man looks at the outward appearance, but the LORD looks at the heart" (1 Sam. 16:7).

Karen has a friend who is like a brother to her and an uncle to her children. Uncle Ray is the pastor of a growing African American church in the inner city. Her family has enjoyed taking in their service and experiencing worship in a way very different from their own church in their small, Midwestern town. As an added bonus, they have been invited to stay for their after-church family-style potluck featuring some of the finest ethnic cuisine this side of heaven! Boxed macaroni and cheese simply won't cut it after sampling the oven-baked, from-scratch fare that the dear sisters at this church are famous for!

HISTORICAL LEADERS—READ ALL ABOUT THEM

The achievements of such leaders as George Washington Carver, Harriet Tubman, and Rev. Martin Luther King Jr. are an important part of our country's history. Take time to learn more about these great Americans.

- A great book that chronicles the escape of African American slaves to the north is *Follow the Drinking Gourd* by Jeanette Winter. Colorful pictures based on American folk tradition vividly help tell this story. Children will learn how runaway slaves used a song taught to them by Peg Leg Joe, a white sailor, to guide them to the Ohio River and ultimately to the Underground Railroad. They were urged to "follow the drinking gourd" (the Big Dipper) to freedom. Read this tale out loud to your children and discuss the issue of slavery in our country. You may also read together various portions of Scripture with those old enough to understand, such as John 15:12–17; Romans 12:3–6; and Galatians 3:28.

- *Amos Fortune: Free Man* by Elizabeth Yates is a touching true story of a slave captured in Africa at the age of fifteen and sold in America in the early 1700s. Amos was a Christian man with godly character. At the age of sixty, he bought his freedom, and then he bought the freedom of several others in the years to follow.

- Another story for young children, *Sweet Clara and the Freedom Quilt* by Deborah Hopkinson, chronicles the life of a young slave girl who creates a patchwork quilt that maps the route leading to the Underground Railroad.

- Get ahold of Martin Luther King Jr.'s famous "I Have a Dream" speech. Gather 'round a table and take turns reading the speech out loud. Discuss what it might have felt like to be an African American at the time in the 1960s when he gave this talk.

President's Day

Celebrate our American heritage by setting aside this special day to remember the presidents of our great nation. We can help our families to be grateful for godly men such as George Washington and Abraham Lincoln, as well as remember our current president. Here are some ideas to help you celebrate this day.

- Read a book about one of the presidents.
- Use coins to help teach young children about the presidents.
- Children can decorate the dinner table in red, white, and blue. (Purchase some Fourth of July paper products when it goes on clearance after the summer holidays.)
- Create a menu using red, white, and blue food.
- End dinner with a special prayer for the president of the United States and our government leaders (see 1 Tim. 2:1–2).

6

MAKE BIRTHDAYS BRIGHT

· · · · · · · · · · · · · · · ·

CAKES AND CANDLES,
PRESENTS AND PARTIES

*For you created my inmost being; you knit me together in my
mother's womb.*

PSALM 139:13

hile you try to show those around you that you love them every day of the
year, there is one day in particular to pull out all the stops—let them take
center stage and be the star of the show. Happy birthday!

HOMESPUN BIRTHDAY PARTIES

Children's birthday parties today seem to be less than old-fashioned. They are usually held outside the home at the newest and coolest playland or restaurant. It seems that to keep up with the neighbors, parents try to make each party bigger and better than the last. Yes, your child's birthday is important, but how do you celebrate in healthy and wholesome ways? How, in a world of keeping up with the Joneses, do you keep children from wanting a bigger and better party year after year? Here are some ideas we've used in our family to help our children appreciate their big day without cramping the family budget.

As parents, choose which years you will celebrate with a big party (friends) and which years will be with just the family. The schedule our family uses is this: the first birthday is celebrated with family and extended family. The second birthday might include a couple of young friends for the birthday boy or girl. The fifth, eighth, tenth, thirteenth, sixteenth, and eighteenth birthdays are certainly milestones in a child's life and so are celebrated with a party including the child's close friends. (Some families choose the twelfth birthday instead of the thirteenth, as the child begins the season of adolescence.) The perfect number of friends to include seems to be between five and ten—enough for fun, but not so many that you break the bank. Celebrate the years in between with just family.

Keep a schedule so birthday boys and girls will keep anticipating that next milestone in his or her life. This also maintains fairness in a family of many children. Since children get so many material things these days, work to ward off the selfish attitude that can develop when so many presents are given to them year after year.

Keep the party simple. Why not celebrate at home, for instance, even if it means having many children in a small house? Or, if you expect comfortable weather, why not outside in the backyard or, with the right theme and decorations, even your garage? Center the main decorations on the party table.

Encourage children to pick a theme that has stood the test of time. Stay away from the latest fads and do a more general theme like baseball, fishing, or dolls.

Choose a gift for the child that centers on the theme of the party. My son who loves fishing received some fishing equipment at his fishing party. My daughter received her first Raggedy Ann and Andy dolls from her grandmothers for her second birthday.

Make your own cake. It really doesn't take much time but can be even more special because you've created it. Year after year my children typically choose the same flavor of cake. Since my birthday is in December, I remember that my mother always made a white cake drizzled with layers of red and green gelatin, frosted with Cool Whip, and decorated with green and red sprinkles. My children love to help design the decorations for their cake. If you have an older child, let him or her bake the cake. It doesn't have to be perfect—but it means so much more when made at home.

Always plan on games that involve children. For little children, one or two games is plenty. It isn't necessary to have prizes for the winners; let them all take home a thank-you bag.

The length of the party will depend on the child's age. For a young child (under five), an hour to an hour and a half will be plenty of fun; they'll lose attention or get fussy after that.

Let the birthday child help choose a small thank-you gift for the children attending the party. Try to stay away from the cheap party-store toys that end up cluttering one's house and usually are lost, broken, or in the garbage within days. Use this principle: one nice thing is better than many cheap things. Choose a small gift that carries out the theme of the party. I found a really nice tackle box at a dollar store, and my son filled it with gummy worms and candy fish for his fishing party. For my daughter's Raggedy Ann party, I found a nice Raggedy Ann and Andy coloring book for under a dollar.

So when planning your child's next birthday party, remember, simple is best. And home is even better!

Kelly

Noah's Ark Party

For a charming party theme based on one of the most beloved stories from the Old Testament, have a Noah's ark birthday party for your little one.

BEFORE THE FLOOD

Copy the invitation from page 176, filling in the necessary details of the party. Decorate for the festivities with animals arranged two-by-two. Your main decorating element can be anything from Beanie Babies or animals crafted from construction paper to ink-stamped pairs of animals down the center of a paper table cloth.

CREATE AN UNFORGETTABLE ARK

Fashion a large appliance box like an ark by painting it brown or covering it with grocery sack-colored paper from a large roll. Cut one door in this ark.

At the party have the children gather stuffed animals from all around the house (scatter them beforehand), scavenger hunt style. Then ask the children to bring the animals two-by-two into the ark. Shut the door and create a storm by flickering the lights on and off and making thunder by pounding on pots and pans.

Once the storm has passed, they can bring the animals out and enjoy the birthday feast.

READ THE STORY

Be sure to include a time of reading the story of Noah from the Bible. It's found in Genesis 6:9–9:17, or you can read from a colorful storybook.

PLAY ANIMAL GAMES

Kids love these simple games that reinforce the story and lessons of Noah:

- Tape on the back of each child a piece of paper with the picture of an animal. They must wander around the room asking others yes or no questions to help them guess their animal, such as "Does it fly?" "Is it brown?" "Does it live in the desert?" When they think they have it figured out, they may guess the name of their animal.

- Have the kids use pieces of white poster board, markers, colored glitter, and glue to make a rainbow to remind them that God will never again flood the whole earth. Write Genesis

AT OUR HOUSE

Even a Little Stew Will Do

As my son Zach has grown so have the ideas for his birthday party—always centered around his interests at each age. For his first birthday, we had a train-themed party, complete with a three-dimensional train cake winding around the table. When he turned five, we were on to cowboys, and on his eighth birthday, army men. (No one will forget the camouflage cake with its green, brown, and black icing!)

For his recent twelfth birthday, we celebrated with a Boy Scout theme. The kids at the party were encouraged to build a fort, identify leaves, and learn how to tie different knots—just the things that Zach had learned in Boy Scouts. This was followed by Hobo Dinners (recipe follows) that everyone loved—and which were familiar from many camping outings.

Occasionally we look back over the pictures from each birthday party, seeing our little boy grow and his interests change. What a wonderful chronicle of memories for our family to share.

HOBO DINNERS

- 6 cups roast beef, cooked and chopped
- 6 cups chicken, cooked and chopped
- 6 cups potatoes, chopped and parboiled
- 4 cups onions, chopped
- 4 cups each assorted vegetables such as red and green peppers, zucchini, yellow squash, mushrooms, and tomatoes butter
- assorted seasonings like salt, pepper, seasoned salt, garlic powder, and steak seasoning

Arrange all of the items in bowls assembly-line style on your table or counter. Have each guest take a piece of thick aluminum foil (or a double layer) about 12 inches square. Then they will go down the line, placing whatever meat and vegetables they wish into the middle of the foil square. Season as desired and dot with a little butter. Just make sure not to overfill! You want to be able to wrap the foil around the items and seal tightly into packets. Have the guests write their name on the foil with a marker. Grill or heat in the oven until vegetables are heated through and tender but not mushy—about 30 minutes. Arrange packets on plates and open carefully to enjoy!

9:14–15 across the top of the poster board: "Whenever I bring clouds over the earth and the rainbow appears in the clouds, I will remember my covenant between me and you and all living creatures of every kind. Never again will the waters become a flood to destroy all life." Then draw a rainbow underneath. Have the children spread glue across one section of the rainbow at a time and then sprinkle on colored glitter. Let dry before giving it to them to take home.

MAKE ENOUGH EATS TO FEED AN ARK

Before you begin to feel like Mrs. Noah, needing to satisfy so many tastebuds at once, read these quick ideas for a festive lunch and snacks. You'll be surprised how quick and easy a Noah's ark party menu can be to pull together.

- Serve blue gelatin in clear plastic cups complete with gummy fish swimming inside. Just let the gelatin set for half the allotted time, place a few fish in, and let set until firm.

- For a main dish, cut lunch meat sandwiches into fun eats by using large animal- or fish-shaped cookie cutters. White bread works best.

- Some specialty grocery and gift stores carry animal-shaped pasta. Use these to make either a pasta salad, macaroni and cheese, or homemade Spaghetti-O's. Simply add spaghetti sauce to your cooked pasta.

- To top the birthday cake, frost with chocolate frosting. Make a ramp out of foil-covered cardboard and lean it into the cake. Make animal crackers enter the ark two-by-two, using little dabs of frosting to secure. Sprinkle coconut dyed blue around the bottom of the cake to serve as the flood waters.

- Animal crackers or Goldfish brand cheese crackers are always a hit.
- Make the following recipes for Easy Elephant Ears and Edible Rainbows to thrill your young partiers.

Easy Elephant Ears

1 17½-ounce package 10-inch tortillas	1½ cups granulated sugar
vegetable oil for frying	1 tablespoon cinnamon

Mix sugar and cinnamon on a large plate and set aside. Over medium heat, heat ¼ cup oil in a skillet or electric frying pan. You'll know the oil is hot when a drop of water sizzles in the oil. Place one tortilla at a time in the oil and cook for 1–2 minutes. When large bubbles form in the tortilla, turn and cook for an additional one minute. Remove from oil and place in sugar mixture, turning to coat. Tastes just like at the carnival!

Edible Rainbows

3–5 6-ounce boxes of gelatin—different colors and flavors
large round glass or metal mixing bowl
whipped cream

Layer various colors and flavors of gelatin in a large glass or metal bowl to form a rainbow. Let each layer set well before adding another. Be sure to let the new layer cool slightly in a separate bowl until semi-set before pouring onto the existing layer—otherwise the new, still-warm liquid gelatin may melt the layer beneath it.

To serve, dip the bowl in warm water for 10–20 seconds, then invert on a serving plate. Slice for a wonderful rainbow effect. Serve individual slices on a cloud of whipped cream. Your little Noah and friends will love this colorful side dish!

Cowboy Party

For the little cowboy (or cowgirl) in your life, have a western party!

For an invitation, make a copy of the WANTED poster from page 173, filling in the necessary information to use as a party invitation.

Decorate western style using bandanas for table runners, western boots to hold silverware, and ropes lassoed around cactus plants for centerpieces.

Make a homemade horse for the little buckaroos to ride! Just take a sawhorse and secure a borrowed saddle to the top. Place a stick horse at the front and secure with rope. Allow enough rope to use the rest as reins.

Encourage western style dress and give each child a sheriff's badge to wear when they arrive.

Play cowboy games like Pin the Tale on the Horse, or have a contest to see who can come up with the most rope tricks.

Watch an old-time western like a Roy Rogers movie or a video of the old *Bonanza* television show.

For cowpoke cuisine, serve chuck wagon chili, cornbread muffins, pasta salad using wagon-wheel shaped pasta, and a cake with a small cactus or cowboy figurine on top. Yee haw!

For a make-and-take project, prepare the fixings for Happy Trail Mix. Place the desired ingredients (see recipe) in a quart-sized reclosable bag with a bandana wrapped around it.

HAPPY TRAIL MIX

Place bowls of the following items in a row on a table. Have children use small paper cups to scoop their favorite items into a quart-sized reclosable bag. You might want to place a limit on the M&M'S, though—they'll go fast!

- dry cereal like Cheerios or Chex
- dried apricots
- granola
- M&M'S, Reese's Pieces, Skittles, or other small chocolate, nutty, and fruity candies
- peanuts
- raisins
- sunflower seeds
- yogurt-covered nuts
- small pretzels

The Princess Parties

Every little girl dreams of becoming a princess. Yet so many girls are being influenced by untrue models telling them who they should be instead of giving them pure and wholesome role models to emulate. Give your precious little girl a beautiful girlhood by using one of these two books as a theme for your princess party.

A PRINCESS IN JESUS'S EYES

This party's theme directs your little girl and her guests to be true princesses in Jesus's eyes. Plan your party using the theme in the children's book *The True Princess* by Angela Elwell Hunt (from Lamplighter Publishing, 1-888-246-7735).

Copy the invitation found on page 178 on parchment paper or cardstock. Lightly color in the illustrations with colored pencils. Roll the invitations up and tie with a ribbon. For a special touch, deliver the invitations by hand to the girls' homes.

Decorations

The colors of your princess party should be lavender, pink, purple, blue, white, and a touch of silver. Using several yards of inexpensive red fabric, lay down a red carpet leading to your front door. Drape a few yards of tulle netting around the front door. Try these royal ideas for table decorations: purchase some silky pink or lavender fabric for the tablecloth; use pretty floral dishes or paperware; scatter colorful, jewel-like beads all over the table; put a vase of fresh-cut flowers in the middle of the table.

Food to Serve

Some fitting meal ideas include cake, mini muffins, breads, cheese, fruit, strawberries dipped in chocolate, and pink lemonade.

Activities

Keep your guests entertained with princess-themed activities:

- As the girls enter the castle, they can begin making a jewel necklace using the beads on the table.
- Read the book *The True Princess* by Angela Elwell Hunt.
- Make princess hats. Shape cardboard or foam sheets (available at craft stores) into a cone shape and insert some tulle through the top of the hat to hang down as far as desired. Glue jewels around the hat.
- As the little princess did in the story, make little pies, and encourage the girls to take them home and give them to someone needy. Share the verses Matthew 20:26–28.

Thank-Yous

Before the girls leave, take a group picture of the girls in their princess hats. Send these with the thank-you cards for the gifts received.

GOD'S GIFT OF PURITY PRINCESS PARTY

This princess party revolves around the book *The Princess and the Kiss: A Story of God's Gift of Purity* by Jennie Bishop (published by Warner Press).

Photocopy the invitation found on page 178 on parchment paper or cardstock. Layer the invitation on top of pretty floral paper cut 1/2 inch larger than the invitation. Add a bow of tulle or ribbon at the top.

Decorations

Use white helium balloons as a sign of purity and white candles to represent light and right. For the table, use white tulle over a white tablecloth and tie large ribbons or strands of smaller ribbons around the edges to hang down. Scatter white or light pink rose petals across the top, with white plate settings and silver flatware. For the centerpiece add a bouquet of white roses, one for each year of the child's age, in a pretty glass vase. Or lay a white rose across each plate. A special touch would be to photocopy the tag featuring 1 Timothy 1:5 found on page 178. Then punch two holes in the tag, one on the left and one on the right. Thread the stem of the white rose through the holes in the sides of the tag.

Music

To set the mood, play a recording of pretty medieval music, such as a harpsichord or harp, during the party.

Food

Serve finger foods such as fruit, cake, and jelly or meat sandwiches on white bread, cut in the shape of a heart using a cookie cutter. Keep the white theme going with 7-Up or white grape juice.

Activities

Read the book *The Princess and the Kiss* by Jennie Bishop. Make a princess veil like the princess in the book. Using white cording, form a circle the size of each girl's head and tie a knot. Take tulle and drape it over the back of the cord to form the veil. Sew or glue the tulle around the cord to secure. Let dry before wearing.

As an alternative, older girls could make roses out of ribbons.

Make white chocolate candy hearts. Simply melt white chocolate chips in the microwave, stirring often. Then pour into heart-shaped candy molds. Let set up in the refrigerator. If these are made at the beginning of the party, they'll be ready to sample before the princesses leave for home.

Take-Home Thank-You Gifts

In a white gift bag, include the following:

- *The Princess and the Kiss: A Story Coloring Book of God's Gift of Purity* (Warner Press) and a box of crayons or colored pencils
- a candy kiss wrapped up in a small piece of tulle, with a tag that says, "God gave the princess a very special gift . . . her first kiss."
- some white rose petals wrapped in tulle, to remind her to keep pure
- the princess veil made at the party
- some of the white chocolate candy hearts

Thank-You Notes

Take a picture of the girls sitting together with their veils. Purchase a white mat for each picture, and under the picture write out 1 Timothy 1:5 in gold pen along with the date. The birthday girl could write her thank-you note on the back of the picture. This would be a nice remembrance of this special day.

The Un-Slumber Pizza Party

When Karen's daughter Mackenzie turned eight, she wanted a slumber party in the worst way. However, some of her friends weren't allowed to spend the night away from home yet. She didn't want them to feel left out, so she came up with a solution. She had an "Un-Slumber" Pizza Party that year instead. Here's how it works:

- Mail each girl a copy of the invitation from page 179.
- Partygoers come dressed in their slumber finery—pajamas, slippers, hair in curlers, etc. Don't forget to have them bring their pillows, sleeping bags, and favorite stuffed animals.
- Play some old-fashioned games like Twister, Scrabble, or Cat's Cradle.
- Watch an age-appropriate movie or tapes of nostalgic shows like *The Brady Bunch*.
- Serve easy snacks like chips, pretzels, and soda pop in cans (kids love to have their own can of pop!). Then make individual pizzas. Let loaves of frozen bread dough thaw, covered, in the fridge overnight. Divide each loaf into three. Let the girls spread out their

piece of dough on a greased cookie sheet. Spread on sauce and cheese. Then let them choose from a variety of toppings to customize their pizza. They may even want to spell out their initials using the toppings in order to keep straight which pizza is theirs! Bake and enjoy!

❧ Instead of a birthday cake, Mackenzie chose Fruit Pizza. It was a big hit. Another idea is Veggie Pizza. Recipes follow.

❧ Be sure to have a "lights out" time near the end of the party when everyone crawls into their sleeping bags and listens to a story on tape. A couple of chapters from *Anne of Green Gables* by L. M. Montgomery would work well.

❧ At the close of the night when parents pick up their kids, they are all ready for bed! Nighty-night!

Fruit Pizza

1 roll of ready-made refrigerated sugar cookie dough (or one batch of your favorite sugar cookie dough recipe, chilled)

8 ounces cream cheese, softened

1 teaspoon vanilla

2 or more cups powdered sugar

assorted fresh fruits—strawberry halves, blueberries, raspberries, mandarin oranges, pineapple tidbits

1/3 cup apple jelly

Spread dough in an ungreased round pizza pan. Bake at 350 degrees for 10–15 minutes or until no longer doughy but not browned. Remove and cool.

Mix cream cheese and vanilla until well blended, using an electric mixer on low speed. Add enough of the sugar to make a spreading consistency. Spread on cooled crust. Top with fruits. You may arrange them in spiral fashion, if desired. Melt the apple jelly in a small pan over low heat. Brush over the fruit to glaze.

Store, covered, in the refrigerator until ready to serve. Placing toothpicks in the pizza and then covering with plastic wrap works best. For a fun presentation, serve in a clean pizza box from your local pizzeria. Be sure to place candles in it for the birthday girl to blow out.

Veggie Pizza

2 packages of crescent rolls

2 8-ounce packages of cream cheese, softened

3/4 cup Miracle Whip or mayonnaise

1 envelope of dry Hidden Valley ranch dressing

3/4 cup each of chopped broccoli, carrots, cauliflower, peppers, onions, and mushrooms

Cover the bottom of a jelly roll pan, pizza pan, or cookie sheet with the crescent rolls, spreading them over the entire pan. Bake at 350 degrees for 8–10 minutes. Cool.

Mix the cream cheese, Miracle Whip or mayonnaise, and dry dressing; spread over crust. Sprinkle vegetables on top, pressing them into the cream cheese mixture. Chill for at least 30 minutes. Cut into slices or bars.

Fishers of Men Party

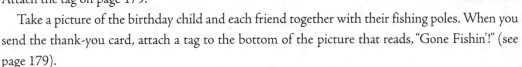

For the little fisherman in your life, create a birthday theme centered on Matthew 4:19: "'Come follow me,' Jesus said, 'and I will make you fishers of men.'"

Send out invitations provided on page 179. Borrow some fishing poles and take your little fisherman and his friends to a local pond or creek to fish. Pack a picnic lunch. Include fish sticks (baked before arrival and eaten first), or tuna fish sandwiches, chips or Goldfish crackers, a cup of blue gelatin with gummy fish, and some blue Kool-Aid. Back at home, serve a Dirt Cake (see the recipe following).

As a thank-you gift, look for a small tackle/tool box at your local dollar store. Fill it with gummy worms, fish candy, Goldfish crackers, and a Go Fish card game. Attach the tag on page 179.

Take a picture of the birthday child and each friend together with their fishing poles. When you send the thank-you card, attach a tag to the bottom of the picture that reads, "Gone Fishin'!" (see page 179).

Dirt Cake

- ½ cup butter, softened
- 1 8-ounce package cream cheese
- ½–1 cup powdered sugar
- 3½ cups milk
- 2 small packages instant vanilla pudding (other flavors may be used)
- 12 ounces frozen whipped topping, partially thawed

- 1 20-ounce package Oreo cookies, crushed
- 1 7-inch flower pot
  gummy worms
  a garden trowel

Mix butter, cream cheese, and sugar with a mixer. In a second bowl, mix pudding and milk. Add whipped topping to the pudding mixture and then combine with the cream cheese mixture.

Cover the bottom of the flower pot with foil. Make several layers of cookie crumbs and cream mixture, ending with cookie crumbs. Cover for several hours in the refrigerator.

Garnish with gummy worms sticking out of the cake. Serve the dessert with a garden trowel.

At Our House

The Birth Day Tale

One of the best ways to create memories for our children when it comes to celebrating their birthdays is to retell the events of the day of their birth.

For our kids, this starts the evening before their big day when I recall to them just what Daddy and I were doing during the hours of the last day we spent without them as a part of our lives. Then I relay to them the first signs of labor that told us they were about to make their grand entrance into the world.

As the day turns to night, I tell bits of information like, "We were on our way to Grandma's house now to drop off your big sister, who was excited to wait for the call from the hospital telling her that you were here!"

Sometimes we try to re-create part of the story. For one child that means a trip to Taco Bell, the last stop we made before my labor started. For another it's a walk around a department store, the place where my husband and I walked to try to get my contractions more regular.

We then sit with their baby pictures from the first weeks of their life and tell them many details:

- what the first few minutes of their lives were like—for two this was rather smooth, but for one rather scary!

- what we were thinking and how we felt as we saw them for the first time

- who came to the hospital to see them and what gifts they were given

- what other names we had considered for them

Our kids simply love to hear the story of their birth, and we make a conscious effort to point them to God and His perfect plan for their lives that all began on that day many (or few) years ago! Those for whom God has chosen to build a family through adoption can use the same concept to tell of the journey of bringing that child into your home, beginning with the desire that was placed in your heart to have a son or a daughter and leading up to the stage where their adoption was final.

Karen

Armor of God

With so many little boys loving to play soldier, here's a way to point them to thinking about God's army—and a great way to minister to a child's friends while you're having fun.

To make invitations, copy the invitation on page 180 featuring Ephesians 6:13. Cut a shield out of poster board a little larger than the invitation. Wrap it with foil to create a shiny look. Glue the invitation on the shield.

Decorate the table with a silver tablecloth. Use red plates and napkins. Put red and silver balloons in the middle of the table.

Have the children sit around the table and offer them a few samples of some plain food that a Roman soldier would have eaten such as bread, cheese, porridge (cream of wheat), hardtack (see recipe on page 38), and grape juice.

Roman soldiers also ate various vegetables and nuts. Put these on a tray and see if the children can guess what they are: garlic, cabbage, nuts, figs, walnuts, lettuces, olives, and leeks.

For a fun activity, let the children make swords. Cut a sword for each child from a heavy piece of cardboard. Let the children wrap the sword in foil to make it a sparkling silver color. On the handle, wrap and tape a piece of black construction paper. Now they are set to have a pretend sword fight.

Give an "Armor of God" play set. This can be your son's first gift to open, and he can then demonstrate for the other children what each piece of armor means by dressing in the armor as you read Ephesians 6:10–18.

Have a race to see who can dress up in the whole armor of God the fastest. Then take a picture of each child dressed in the armor. Be sure to send this along with the thank-you note.

Roman soldiers had to follow strict orders and be obedient to their commanders. Play a game of Simon Says to see who can follow the commands. Let the kids practice marching around the yard like Roman soldiers.

Purchase a poster coloring page of the soldier dressed in his armor by artist Alice Craig (available at www.aliceart.net). These make great take-home gifts for the children.

Grown-Up Gatherings

Maybe you have a special adult in your life who is about to celebrate a birthday. Where do you begin? First of all, look at the life of that individual. What hobbies does he enjoy? What interests does she pursue? Once you think this through, we're sure you'll find the perfect theme to design a birthday party around!

If your loved one plays golf, build a party around that; if it's sewing or quilting, use that theme for your festivities. Design invitations, decorations, and even food around the theme of your choice. Your party could take shape in all kinds of ways. For an outdoorsman, decorate with tents and piles of logs and have s'mores to eat. For an avid reader, make invitations that open like a book, place an assortment of books in stacks around the room to decorate, and serve alphabet soup! Whatever you choose to build your party around, get your imagination going—the possibilities are endless. Here are a few other suggestions to round out the perfect birthday party for an adult.

BE OUR GUEST

Place at the doorway to your home (or in another place everyone must stop and pass through) a blank book or guest book that guests can sign as they arrive. Everyone must also write down a special memory they have of the birthday man or woman.

GET IT IN PICTURES

Have the guests bring copies of any pictures they might have of themselves with the birthday person. These make great conversation starters when placed here and there on tables—the stories will be priceless!

MAKE A FAVORITE MEAL

If the honored guest's mother is still living, have her help you prepare favorite foods from childhood. If mom lives far away, do a little research into favorite foods or get some of mom's recipes and make an extra-special feast!

CREATE A MEMORY LANE

On the invitation, mention that you'd like people to come prepared to share a favorite memory of the birthday guy or gal. Be sure to get these on videotape—to be enjoyed for years to come.

The Birthday Book

If you have someone who is celebrating a milestone birthday such as their thirtieth, fortieth, or even the Big 5-0, surprise them with a birthday book! This will be a cherished conversation piece for years to come. Here's how it works:

Go to the library and check out a copy of *The Address Book: How to Reach Anyone Who Is Anyone*—a reference volume that lists the addresses of famous people, from authors to television actors, radio personalities, movie stars, politicians, and more.

Make up a flyer that says "Happy Birthday to _____ [fill in the name]." Print the needed number of copies.

Then go through *The Address Book* and locate the names and addresses of any famous people your birthday man or woman would love to hear from with a special greeting. Many of these folks have assistants and agencies set up to respond to such fan mail, so send a cover letter letting them know your loved one is having a birthday and would get a huge kick out of receiving a special greeting from them. Encourage them to write a greeting on the enclosed flyer and then mail it back to you in a self-addressed, stamped envelope that you will have provided for them. If the person you are

doing this for lives in your home, route the return letters to the house of a friend or relative who can collect them for you so as not to let the cat out of the bag. You'll have a better chance of getting a response if the flyers reach people three months before the actual birthday.

When the flyers are all in, compile them in a three-ring binder using plastic page protectors. You can also mail copies of the flyer to un-famous but important people in the person's life—friends, relatives, co-workers, neighbors, and former classmates and teachers. As much as they will love to get the greetings from famous folks, the ones from people in their own life will be the most meaningful.

We have implemented this idea in the past with great success. For the most part, about 80 percent of the celebrities have returned the flyers. Some have even included signed 8-by-10-inch glossy pictures and clever greetings, such as Joan Rivers penning the words, "Happy Birthday, Margaret . . . Can we talk?" and Don Ho sending an autographed color picture of himself in all of his Hawaiian splendor.

This is one unique gift that is sure to bring a smile!

The Value of a Gift

Brenda Paccamonti of Normal, Illinois, always gives her niece and nephew money for gifts. "As teenagers, that is really what they want," she says. "But I refuse to give it to them in an ordinary way." So each year, she does something different. Try some of Brenda's quirky ideas!

FROZEN ASSETS

Find the largest container you have that will fit into your freezer; fill it halfway with water and place it in the freezer. Once it is frozen, put a reclosable bag filled with coins on it, fill it the rest of the way with water, and let it freeze. On the big day, your loved one will have fun taking the ice block out to the driveway and chipping at the block of ice with a hammer to get to the money.

FOLDING MONEY

Origami with money is always fun. Try making a wreath with one-dollar bills. Make a circle out of heavy gauge wire, twisting the wire ends together to secure. Tie a 6-inch length of white ribbon around the middle of several dollar bills. Then tie these ends into a bow around the wire farme. Continue working around until the entire frame is full of money. Or try making angels out of your bills. Just fold lengthwise—accordion style. Holding the top, fan out the bottom of the bill. Drill a large hole into the bottom of 1-inch wooden balls (available at craft stores). Tuck the top of the dollar bill into the hole. Decorate the wooden ball with a face, hair, even a halo.

GIVING A FORTUNE

Did you know you can make your own fortune cookies? Fold money up very small and wrap it tightly with plastic wrap. Make fortune cookies using the recipe that follows, putting the money inside the cookies. Present the cookies in a Chinese takeout container. Fun!

Happy Luck Fortune Cookies

20 one-dollar bills (or write messages on about 20 strips of paper)
1 cup flour
2 tablespoons cornstarch
1/2 cup sugar
1/2 teaspoon salt
2 egg whites
1/2 cup vegetable oil
1 teaspoon water
2 teaspoons vanilla extract

Tips before starting: make only two or three cookies at a time, because the cookies become stiff very quickly and when cooled are too brittle to bend into their familiar shape. To form into the crescent shape, you'll need a muffin pan. To handle the hot cookies, wear cotton gloves.

Preheat the oven to 300 degrees. In a large bowl sift together the flour, cornstarch, sugar, and salt. Stir in the egg whites, oil, water, and vanilla. Divide dough into 20 balls. On a greased surface, roll each ball into a very thin circle of dough. Then place two or three at a time on a well-greased baking sheet. Bake for 15 minutes or until golden.

Remove one cookie at a time from the baking sheet with a wide spatula. Working quickly, follow these four steps:

1. Flip cookie onto cotton-gloved hand.
2. Hold fortune (or money) in center of pliable cookie while folding cookie in half.
3. Grasp ends of cookie and draw ends gently together to form a crease at center of cookie.
4. Fit cookie in muffin cup (points down) to hold shape as it cools. If cookie hardens too quickly, put it back in the oven for about 1 minute.

Repeat for as many cookies as dough makes. Store cookies in an airtight container.

A PICTURE OF PROSPERITY

Use cardboard to make a lovely but inexpensive—and personal—picture frame on which you can write a message. Decorate the frame with your money gift by hot gluing quarters all the way around.

BANK ON IT

Put some money inside a papier-mâché piggy bank for your little investors. You can doll up the pig as much as you like, complete with eyelashes, fancy bow, and painted toenails.

A TRICK AND TREAT

For Halloween, look for packaged candy in small boxes. Empty out each box, put a dollar inside, and glue the lid shut again. Then wrap each one individually and send your little loved ones a real treat—with a twist and a trick too!

Miscellaneous Memories

Charlie smiled nervously and sat down on the edge of the bed. He was holding his present, his only present, very carefully in his two hands. WONKA'S WHIPPLE-SCRUMPTIOUS FUDGEMALLOW DELIGHT, it said on the wrapper.

CHARLIE AND THE CHOCOLATE FACTORY
BY ROALD DAHL

Perhaps you can't celebrate every birthday with a big party, but you'd still like to make the day special. Try some of these ideas for birthday memories!

WHILE THEY'RE SLEEPING

Jill Savage of Normal, Illinois, has a fun birthday tradition in her family. During the night on the eve of a family member's birthday, the rest of the clan sneaks into their room and decorates it with streamers, posters, and balloons. When morning comes, the special birthday boy or girl is greeted with a newly decorated room, and then the entire family troops downstairs to eat their traditional birthday breakfast—cake and ice cream!

YOUR TURN, YOUR DAY

Renee Schafer of DeWitt, Michigan, spoils each of her children on their birthdays. They get to pick whatever they want to eat the entire day and have at least one friend over. They are honored on their special day and given total freedom from chores. They get balloons on the Special Birthday Chair, cake, gifts, games, and gobs of attention! Then the family talks about the day they were born and ends by thanking God in prayer for this precious jewel.

ORDERED "TO GO"

Pamper your birthday girl or guy by allowing them to order their birthday meals! The day before the big day, place a copy of the door hanger from page 175 on their door. Just like at a hotel, they can circle and choose their favorite breakfast items for their favorite day. Then they put the hanger back on the door for Mom to pick up. This also gives Mom a little extra time to shop and prepare!

A STATE OF CELEBRATION!

For an out-of-the-ordinary kind of birthday celebration, get together with another family or two and celebrate your state's birthday!

Hop on the Internet or hit the books at your local library and find out interesting facts about your state. Be sure to discover just when it was admitted to the Union, any resources your state is known for, and any particular foods that are native to your neck of the woods. Then make a Happy Birthday banner, whip up some food, and get ready to celebrate! In our case, living in Michigan, we would hold our party on January 26, the date that Michigan entered the Union way back in 1837. You could even give a short trivia quiz about well- and little-known facts about your state. This way you not only have a party to participate in, but you sneak in a little history lesson as well. Happy birthday to your star on the flag!

7

CELEBRATE THE MILESTONES

. . . .

BRIDES AND BLESSINGS,
ANNIVERSARIES AND ADOPTIONS

From the fullness of his grace we have all received one blessing after another.

JOHN 1:16

Your niece's bridal shower, Grandma and Grandpa's fiftieth wedding anniversary, the birth of your cousin's first child—as you turn each page of your calendar, occasions for celebrations abound. Let us help you make the most of these outstanding occasions.

Bridal Shower Blessings

I don't want a fashionable wedding, but only those
about me whom I love, and to them I wish to look
and be my familiar self.

MEG IN *LITTLE WOMEN*
BY LOUISA MAY ALCOTT

Today, bridal showers are typically a one-time thing where family and
friends get together to shower the bride-to-be with gifts for her new home.
The bride and groom usually create a gift registry and choose specific items
they would like in their home, even specifying the color, size, amount, and
quantity desired. At many of these showers, the gifts are no surprise to the
bride or guests.

If your daughter is getting married, several months before the wedding
plan monthly showers of blessings leading up to the wedding date. If there
are sisters or sisters-in-law, they could help in the hospitality. Invite a group
of family members, friends, and godly women from your church for evenings
of fellowship and encouragement—showering your daughter with different
blessings each month to help prepare her home. This can also be a time to
lift up prayer for your daughter, the groom, the wedding preparations, the
ceremony, and the marriage. A different woman each time would be asked
to share a devotional on marriage. Each shower would have a different
theme and each of the guests would bring one small item each time for a
gift, instead of one larger gift. Some ideas for the showers include:

Recipe Shower: Each guest brings her favorite recipe written on a recipe card and then shares
why it is a family favorite or where it came from. Each person could prepare the recipe for a potluck
for all to enjoy. As a special gift, the mother of the bride can choose a special recipe box to give her
daughter that already includes all the family favorite recipes. Long ago, recipes were not just a list of
ingredients but precious heirlooms passed down through generations.

Linens Shower: Items given can be anything that is made from fabric. Something homemade
would be extra special. Ideas include bath towels, a quilt (maybe one Grandma made or an heirloom),
doilies, a tea cozy, and kitchen towels.

Pantry Shower: Guests are asked to bring one item for the couple's pantry. These could consist of
baking powder, baking soda, salt, sugar, oil, tea, vinegar, and others. The bride's mom could prepare
a list of staples her daughter could use as a resource to stock her pantry.

Candle Shower: Each guest brings a candle for the bride. Be sure to create atmosphere with candlelight and some light refreshments.

Paper/Organization Shower: Each guest brings a paper item that will help the young bride organize her new home. Gifts could include shopping lists, calendar, address book, envelopes, stationery, stamps, or a box of cards. Then have each guest give the bride a great tip on organization they have learned in their life.

Homemade Shower: Showers these days usually do not contain many gifts that were homemade as in the past. Each guest can bring some simple item they have made to make the couple's new home feel cozy and warm.

Planning a blessing of showers before the wedding will most importantly encourage your daughter to glean wisdom from godly women as she takes on the new role of being a wife.

THE KITCHEN SHOWER: WHAT'S COOKIN'?

For a kitchen shower guests can bring one kitchen utensil such as a spatula, whisk, small kitchen scale, cookie cutters, or rolling pin. The utensils don't need to be expensive, just essential to the young bride.

For a unique bridal shower that is sure to tickle the taste buds, expand on this idea. Based on Psalm 34:8, "Taste and see that the Lord is good; blessed is the man who takes refuge in him," this shower can be designed to stock the bride's kitchen cabinets and recipe box.

Using the invitation on page 181 or creating one of your own, instruct guests to bring a kitchen utensil or dish as their gift. In addition to the invitation, send them a blank recipe card (see page 181) or a blank 3-by-5 index card. They must also bring a handwritten recipe on the card provided. But the catch is that the gift must be an item that will be used in the recipe. For example, if someone is giving a pie plate, they could write out their famous peach pie recipe.

If desired, you could also have the guests bring their recipe already prepared, providing the bride (and guests) a sampling of what could be created in her kitchen. Have a recipe card box provided at the door for people to slip their recipe inside.

For delightful decorations, place vintage tablecloths around the room on tables and over the backs of chairs. These tablecloths provide a colorful, cheerful backdrop for your festivities as well as unique conversation starters.

A few weeks ahead of time, scout antique stores (or your own attic!) for the perfect accents to complete your decorations. Look for old vegetable peelers, graters, and utensils. How about using an aged muffin tin filled with votive candles as a decoration or an old soup pot to supply napkins? Try using old-fashioned jars for centerpieces. Simply fill with fresh flowers, beans, or pasta—anything goes!

IT'S ABOUT TIME

Rather than holding a traditional bridal shower, try an Around-the-Clock Shower instead. Use the invitation from page 180. On the invitations, assign each guest a time of the day: 8:00 a.m., 12:00 noon, 4:00 p.m., 10:00 p.m., and so on.

The guest then needs to purchase a gift the bride will use at that time of the day. For the morning perhaps an appropriate gift would be a waffle maker; for late afternoon, a frying pan for her to start supper with; or for a late night assignment, a pretty nightgown. You can even decorate using various old-fashioned alarm and mantle clocks. Serve recipes with thyme as an ingredient, such as Herbed Chicken Salad and a fresh salad with Thyme Vinegar and Oil salad dressing.

Herbed Chicken Salad

6	cups cooked, cubed chicken breast
1	cup diced celery
1/2	cup finely chopped purple onion
1 1/2	cups frozen peas, thawed and drained
2	cups pineapple tidbits, drained
2 1/2	cups mayonnaise
2	tablespoons vinegar
1/4	cup sugar
1/2	teaspoon salt
3	tablespoons fresh or 2 teaspoons dried thyme (lemon thyme is nice)
2	cups lightly salted cashews
	lettuce leaves, for serving

Combine first five ingredients in a large bowl. In a small bowl, mix together mayonnaise, vinegar, sugar, salt, and thyme. Pour over chicken mixture and combine well. Just before serving, add cashews. Serve on lettuce leaves. Serves eight.

Thyme Vinegar and Oil Dressing

1 cup olive oil
$^1/_2$ cup cider vinegar
$^1/_2$ teaspoon salt
$^1/_2$ teaspoon dry mustard
$^1/_4$ teaspoon garlic powder
1 teaspoon dried basil
1 teaspoon dried sage
1 teaspoon dried thyme
pinch of black pepper
1 $^3/_4$-ounce package of Good Seasons Garlic and Herb Salad Dressing Mix

Blend all ingredients thoroughly in a small bowl. Serve over fresh greens for a refreshing beginning to your meal.

SEW NICE!

Many women today either don't know how to sew or don't have the tools they need when it comes time to patch up a pair of holey jeans or sew on a loose button. Help them out! The next time you help give a wedding shower, ask the guests to bring one small item to fill the bride's sewing basket. Just search through your local fabric store for anything small and useful—thread, a small pair of scissors, a pack of needles, even rickrack or zippers. Then at the shower you can provide a nice sewing basket for the bride. Set it out near the door so that the guests can tuck their contribution inside when they arrive. Then at the end of the festivities, present this sewing kit to the bride. She'll think you're all *sew nice*!

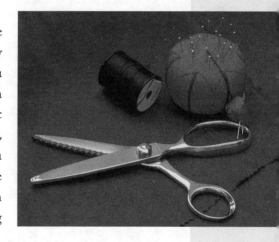

BUDGET BASKET

For a new couple just beginning their journey together, give them a budget basket! Fill a sturdy, practical woven basket with a calculator, pens, a ledger tablet, and a book on budgeting.

Good book choices include Mary Hunt's *Debt-Proof Your Marriage* or Larry Burkett's *The Family Financial Workbook*. Burkett includes a comprehensive collection of easy-to-follow, reproducible worksheets to help get a budget started. Financial advisor Ron Blue's *Master Your Money* also combines the Bible's timeless teachings on stewardship and responsibility with up-to-date advice on financial management and cash control; the book includes easy-to-follow charts, worksheets, and a handy glossary of terms. These books are designed to help a couple come up with, and stick to, a budget.

Fill in the rest of the basket with play paper money, gold foil-wrapped chocolate coins, and snack-sized Payday or 100 Grand candy bars.

Wrap the basket up in clear cellophane and tie shut with a bright green ribbon. Add the tag from page 183 featuring the verse, "Give me neither poverty nor riches, but give me only my daily bread" (Prov. 30:8).

CLEANING CADDY

For a housewarming gift for a new neighbor or brand-new bride, give her a cleaning caddy! Fill a large plastic carrying tote or cleaning bucket with the following items:

- household sponges
- soap-filled steel wool pads
- a bottle of floor cleaner
- some furniture polish
- a bottle of glass cleaner
- some all-purpose cleaner
- rubber cleaning gloves
- cotton dust rags
- a copy of a good book on cleaning

Books like *Living Organized* and *Simply Organized* by Sandra Felton are good for every home. *Speed Cleaning* by Jeff Campbell teaches a method of cleaning that saves time while cleaning thoroughly. Here's another fun book: *Is There Life after Housework?* by Don Aslett will be inspiring for tackling the nasty chore of housecleaning with enthusiasm.

You can also include some rewards for a job well done. Fine chocolates or a pound of her favorite coffee are good choices. Be sure to photocopy and tie on a copy of the Scripture tag from page 183 featuring the verse, "Create in me a clean heart, O God" (Ps. 51:10 KJV).

MORE BRIDAL BASICS

Whatever theme, locale, or type of shower you choose, these ideas will help you pull off a great event to be remembered and treasured.

Book of Blessings

As guests arrive for a shower, have a new address book and pen available at the door for them to fill out. Just have them turn to the appropriate section and fill out their name and address. Also have thank-you notes and envelopes set out nearby. Have guests fill out an envelope with their name and address. This will make things so much easier for the bride as she simply fills out the thank-yous and tucks them into the correct envelope.

Picture Perfect Decor

For a bridal shower decorating idea, locate copies of pictures of the bride-to-be and her soon-to-be husband in days gone by. Using double-sided tape, secure pictures back to back, pairing snapshots of them at about the same age. Or you may want to secure these to a piece of card stock paper that has been cut out with decorative edged scissors. Then float the pictures around the room by attaching them with tape to the ribbon on a helium balloon. You may need to experiment with the best place to secure the pictures to the ribbon so they will float. Guests will have fun viewing the happy couple at various stages in their lives.

Get the Newlyweds Cooking

To fill the bride's spice rack, have all of the guests bring a spice that begins with the same letter as their own name. For example, Suzy might bring sage, Mary bring marjoram, and Trish bring thyme. Some of your guests might have to get a little creative to find spices that begin with the first letter of their name, but the bride will be able to cook some amazing creations with her fully stocked spice rack!

Dress the Bride, More or Less

For a game that is sure to bring some laughs and make memories, divide the bridal shower guests into teams of four or five. Give each group a few rolls of toilet tissue. Let them select one person to serve as the bridal model. Then have the groups use the tissue to craft a wedding gown on that person. When everyone is finished, the bride-to-be picks her favorite gown and the team members all receive a prize!

Happy Anniversary

To celebrate your anniversary when there are children in the house, get them in on the fun too. Get out your wedding photo album to flip through or video to watch. For dinner make a dish that was served at your reception. If you were married far away, get out a map and show them the location of the town in which you were wed.

Here are some ideas for celebrating the anniversary of friends or family.

LET EVERYONE DISH

For a couple celebrating a milestone such as a fortieth or fiftieth wedding anniversary, instead of having a fancy, catered affair, have each of their children make a dish to pass that they remember having during their growing-up days. Food, fun, and memories!

RENEW VOWS

For a get-together for your church family, hold a renewing of your vows ceremony. Have couples sign up ahead of time, giving their wedding date. Plan food for the reception and order a wedding cake. Couples can invite guests like children and relatives; then let the ceremony begin.

Have guests seated, candles lit, flowers in place. Couples walk down the aisle starting with the most recently married on down to the pair that has been together the longest. After a brief ceremony, head to the reception to enjoy the food and look at each other's wedding photo albums. If your own pastor and his wife would like to participate, have a pastor from a nearby or sister church officiate. You could even encourage ladies to wear their wedding dress if it still fits! Hold the ceremony in June or near Valentine's Day. What a wonderful way to celebrate God's gift of marriage!

Welcome to Our World

Sons are a heritage from the LORD, children
a reward from him.

PSALM 127:3

Family and friends rally around to rejoice in the birth or arrival of each new little one. As your family circle grows bigger and stronger, let us help you celebrate these joyous occasions with the following ideas.

SIBLING REVELRY

Often the anticipation of a new baby can leave older siblings feeling left out. If your daughter, sister, or close friend is expecting a new little one, ask if you can borrow the sibling(s) for help in planning, decorating, and celebrating a new one on the way.

They can help you plan the menu. Even if it takes a little extra time, allow them to help you prepare the food. Let them stir the punch or place silverware on the table. The more they are involved, the more excited they will be.

Ask them if they'd like to greet guests as they arrive. If the child is old enough to write, have him or her sit next to Mom and record what gifts she receives and who they are from.

Have a special T-shirt printed just for the sibling to wear at the shower. "I'm going to make a great big sister!" printed on a pretty pink shirt will make any sister-to-be feel extra special.

POPCORN PRAYER

During the shower have a time of prayer for the new baby—where anyone who desires may jump in with their thoughts, wishes, and prayers for the new one on the way.

ACROSTIC GREETINGS

If the baby has already arrived or you at least know the name the parents have picked out for their precious bundle, you can make a beautiful table decoration that will find an honored place in the baby's room.

Just pick out verses from the Bible—verses that will illustrate a character trait for each letter of the baby's name. For instance, for the name Adam, you might choose these verses:

A—"Your ATTITUDE should be the same as that of Christ Jesus" (Phil. 2:5)

D—"The desires of the DILIGENT are fully satisfied" (Prov. 13:4)

A—"Do your best to present yourself to God as one APPROVED, a workman who does not need to be ashamed and who correctly handles the word of truth" (2 Tim. 2:15)

M—"What does the Lord require of you? To act justly and to love MERCY and to walk humbly with your God" (Mic. 6:8)

WORDS OF WISDOM

As the guests arrive for the shower, place a journal on a table near the door, already prepared with dividers or different sections for them to share their thoughts and ideas on the following topics: potty training, teething, sleepless nights, illness, childproofing, must-have baby items. For a new mom, the more information, the better!

AT OUR HOUSE

Sweet Dreams Are Made of This

When our children were younger they enjoyed both decorating for holidays and surprising their family. So on our fifteenth wedding anniversary, they decorated their bedroom with streamers and signs, then proudly invited us in. As we entered the room, they yelled, "Surprise! Happy anniversary! You get to sleep with us!" They had transformed their bedroom into our anniversary suite, complete with children sleeping at our sides. And that's just what we did!

Karen Andrews, DeWitt, Michigan

AT OUR HOUSE

The Shower without Mom or Baby

When my friends approached me about hosting our baby shower, I was delighted! I'd been sewing, decorating, and trying as best I could to prepare for my first baby, but I knew I did not have everything I needed.

"But," I said, "could we wait and have the shower after the baby is born? That way the guests could see the baby and the gifts would be just right for whatever this baby turns out to be." My friends agreed that it was a wonderful idea, and they started to plan a lovely day full of food and fellowship a full two weeks after I was expected to deliver.

When the long-anticipated due date came and went with no results, I wasn't worried—there was still plenty of time before the shower was scheduled. I did, however, become more concerned as days passed and still no baby!

Finally, a full ten days after he was expected, my son Zachariah arrived. *Still plenty of time*, I thought. I wasn't counting on recuperation from a cesarean section, though. There was no time to stop the party now, though—food had been ordered, invitations sent, and decorations gathered! What were we to do?

As it turned out, Zach and I missed our shower—we were actually traveling home from the hospital as it was going on. As we drove by our church, we could see all the cars parked in neat little rows. But on we went—because we were such new parents, we wouldn't have dreamed of stopping in to show our new bundle off. We had to get the little one home!

How can you have a baby shower with neither guest of honor present?

Well, one member of the family traveled down to the hospital to take some video of the new baby. This video was played on a TV set at the shower, so there was Zach displayed on camera for all to see! Pictures were passed around the room as well. The guests could discuss which of his parents he resembled more and how cute he was. My husband and I were also able to give a personal thank-you message to those who attended. Soon after my new little family arrived home, the presents were delivered, along with a full report of the day. I think all the guests enjoyed this one-of-a-kind baby shower.

Trish

GIVE THEM ROOTS

For a lasting reminder of the birth of that precious little one, plant a tree when your baby is born. As the years go by and they grow together, be sure to get pictures of the child next to the tree. From a schoolchild hanging from its limbs to a young married man standing under its sheltering branches, what a great chronicle of God's creation!

SHOWER POWER

For a fun baby shower game, have the guests attending bring a picture of themselves as babies. Place them up on a piece of poster board with a number by each of them. Pass out pencils and paper. Then try to guess which person's name corresponds with each baby photo. Give a prize to the person who gets the most answers right.

For a quick and easy shower game idea, have guests bring a jar of baby food that begins with the same letter as either their first or last name. For example, Pam would bring pears, and Mrs. Smith would bring sweet potatoes (or a sweet potato pie, knowing Mrs. Smith!). When the mom-to-be returns home, she'll have a stash of baby food for when her little one starts eating solids.

For a hilarious game at a baby shower, purchase jars of baby food. Remove the labels and then have a "taste testing" contest. Is it squash or carrots? Pears or peas? How can babies stand this stuff?

For a new twist on an old stand-by game, have the mom-to-be walk around the room carrying a tray full of baby items: diaper pins, baby shampoo, teething gel, a rattle, booties, a pacifier. Make sure there are at least twenty items on the tray. Tell guests to look very carefully at what they see. Then have the mom-to-be leave the room. Guests will think you are going to have them write down everything that was on the tray. Instead, have them write down everything the mom-to-be was wearing! Award a prize for the most correct answers.

If a baby has already been born, have the guests make as many words as they can out of the letters in the baby's first, middle, and last name.

AWESOME ADOPTIONS!

> He settles the barren woman in her home as a happy mother of children.
>
> PSALM 113:9

Families can grow in so many ways. But one extraordinary way families expand is by opening their homes to children that they did not give birth to. These special people are all around us, inviting children who may not have anywhere else to go into their homes and hearts. No matter how a family has grown, whether through birth or adoption, the arrival of each child is a blessed event. Here are some suggestions for celebrating the coming of a child into your circle of friends and family. Whether you've adopted or just want to show your support to someone who has, you can rejoice in the special way a family has found each other!

If an older child joins your family, explore with them some of the traditions and foods they were used to. Then work to incorporate everything you can into your own celebrations. Since they have left everything they knew, it's great to give them back something familiar.

Adoptions involving children from other countries are on the rise. Why not give them the gift of their heritage? Present a gift that represents the country the child was born in. When you celebrate your child's adoption, include foods from the country they came from.

If you haven't adopted but you know someone who has, educate your own family about adoption and what it means. This could mean talking over with your children appropriate adoption language and questions to ask. For instance, we say, "birth mother" instead of "real mother." More examples can be found by searching the Internet for "positive adoption language."

Read books about adoption with your children: *A Mother for Choco* by Keiko Kasza is a great story about a bird who is searching for a mother but finds a whole family. *Just a Little Different* by Gina and Mercer Mayer

AT OUR HOUSE

The Real Birthday Gift of Adoption

Because my children are adopted and do not share the same race, we look very different from each other. But that is our gift every day. When I see the differences in us, I also see the sovereignty of God—and it is then that I realize we were intended for each other. That is the true celebration of adoption and how wondrous and truly awesome it is to ponder how, even though each child was formed inside another woman, they had already become ours!

Cyndi Thelen, Saint Johns, Michigan

tells the tale of Lil' Critter as he makes a new friend whose family is just a little different. Offer to read one of these books in your child's classroom at school, or donate a book about adoption to your school or local library.

Plan an open house following your child's finalization hearing. Family and friends will love the chance to rejoice, celebrate, and support you!

Start with a Key and a Clean House

Many times children are placed in adoptive or foster homes without much if any notice. You can help! Get a key from the prospective parents and plan a special homecoming. If the house needs cleaning, take along your cleaning supplies. Provide a meal for the new family. Make a banner welcoming the new family member, whether young or older. Balloons, stuffed animals, confetti—all these will add to the festive atmosphere of this outstanding occasion.

AT OUR HOUSE

A Fresh Start

I was fifteen years old when a friend of the family told my sister and me that we were moving to Michigan to live with an aunt and uncle. Though we had known this aunt and uncle all our lives, we'd only seen them at most once a year.

It was a scary prospect to leave friends and familiar places to travel to a distant place and live with people we hardly knew. I remember packing a box full of clothes and what other belongings I had and heading into the unknown. I was sure glad that at least I had a sister to sympathize with.

When we arrived at our new home, we were shown our rooms and allowed to settle in. The next day it was off to school to sign up for classes and begin the process of meeting teachers and making friends. It was difficult to merge two girls into new sets of rules, new family traditions, new "parents." But the love and flexibility of my aunt and uncle gradually helped us feel that we really were home. Memories that we made together—Sunday dinners, family vacations, Christmas cookies—all contributed to our sense of belonging.

Thanks, Aunt Fran and Uncle Barry, for opening your home and hearts to a pair of girls who needed a home!

Trish

Document the Days

Take pictures of the new family arriving home. These can be used in later years to help the child realize how very excited everyone was at their arrival.

Or make a scrapbook to have ready and waiting for the new arrival. Display and label family photos with names and relationships. For older children, this can be invaluable—remember, they must get to know a whole new family!

Give Mom a Break

Remember that every new mom, whether or not she has given birth to a baby, may still experience sleepless nights! Why not give her a Mom's Day Off? Just offer to take care of the children for a while so she has time for herself, to go shopping, to take a leisurely walk, even for an uninterrupted nap. If the child joining the family is older, offer to take him or her out for ice cream or pizza so Mom can catch up on housework or rest.

Drive the Welcome Wagon—By Basket

Many times foster and adoptive children come into new homes without certain necessities. Why not give a special gift basket to the new arrival?

For a baby include diapers, wipes, pacifiers, bottles, and maybe a new outfit.

For older children make up a basket containing undergarments, socks, stuffed animals, a special nightlight, toothbrush, toothpaste, pajamas, sheets (of their very own!), and age-appropriate books, music, and videos. For girls, add hair accessories, soaps, lotions, and other hygiene products. For boys, include Legos, K'nex, crayons—anything to help keep little hands busy. These little items will be greatly appreciated!

CELEBRATE YOUR FAITH

. . . .

RITES AND RITUALS,
PURITY AND PRAYER

Your statutes are my heritage forever;
they are the joy of my heart.

PSALM 119:111

As a church body, we commemorate many aspects of the Christian life: the birth of our Lord; His crucifixion, death, and burial; and especially His glorious and victorious resurrection. In the life of the body we also find many causes for celebration in community. When one is baptized or added to the membership of the church, when a missionary leaves for the field, or when a young couple enters the ministry, we have cause to rejoice with them. This corporate celebration brings us closer as a church and is a huge source of encouragement for the one who is at the center of the excitement.

In much the same way, each of us belongs to another body—the church within your four walls. Just as we celebrate as a large group, we find cause for celebration on a smaller but no less grand scale when a member of our own family reaches a goal or passes a spiritual milestone. In this chapter you will find ideas to aid in the rejoicing. Whether it is an event in the life of a fellow churchgoer or of a member of your own household, we hope you will be able to implement some of these concepts to make the occasion even more memorable. What a wonderful way to "rejoice with those who rejoice" (Rom. 12:15)!

Setting Apart Sundays

Christians can learn much from a study of the way the Jewish people celebrate the Sabbath each week. We hope the following mini-lesson on the Sabbath and some corresponding Sunday ideas will help you and your family to have restful, worshipful times on the Lord's Day.

We just love the picture painted in the musical *Fiddler on the Roof*: it is about twenty minutes before sundown. Everyone is rushing and hustling as the chores are finished, delicious food is prepared, and special Sabbath dishes are put out. The children drop coins for the poor into a box as one of them runs to the window to check the position of the setting sun in the sky.

Just as the sun begins to set, the family takes their places around the table. The mother in the family lights two candles: one to remember the Sabbath, and one to keep it holy. They ting a little bell announcing the arrival of Queen Sabbath, the special guest that they have been waiting for all week. Then they are off to attend a service at the synagogue.

Returning home, the father has a custom of laying his hands on each child and pronouncing a blessing in accordance with Numbers 6:24–27. He also blesses his wife by quoting from the book of Proverbs, chapter 31. They say a prayer called the Kiddush over wine and two loaves of Challah bread, a beautiful, sweet, braided bread that is kept hidden under a cloth until ready to be revealed. They then eat a meal consisting of chicken soup, fish, and beef. Then they are off to bed. Early the next morning, they attend a three-hour service followed by a time of "noshing," which means snacking and fellowship. They then return home to rest, read, eat, and nap, and finally they attend a late afternoon service where the rabbi pronounces the Havdalah prayer. Havdalah means division. The idea is that they are now dividing as a congregation and going back out to the world where, at the end of another week, they will meet again for the Sabbath. There is actually a sadness that the day is over and Queen Sabbath is leaving. Finally, forty minutes after sundown, it is all over.

The Jewish people actually order their week around the Sabbath. Instead of "Thank God It's Friday," they are most excited for the Sabbath to arrive. They spend three days in anticipation and then three days looking back at what God taught them on that day. We can take our cue from them by trying hard to have housework done, bills paid, and the laundry put away so we can spend our Sundays resting, worshiping, and being with others instead of trying to play catch-up!

The Sabbath is meant to be holy. Holy means set apart or different. Here are some ideas to help your Sunday, the Lord's Day, be set apart and different.

FAMILY GAMES, TOYS, AND BOOKS

Have toys with spiritual connotations that are only to be played with on Sundays—perhaps a Bible trivia game, an Armor of God play set, a Noah's Ark set, or a few Christian videos. Read aloud some books about great missionaries or some Christian fiction. Our families have enjoyed the Frank Peretti mystery series for kids. Tapes of *Adventures in Odyssey* radio shows work well too to get your little ones settled in for a nap.

TRADITIONS

It doesn't matter what you do, just that your kids have a recollection of you doing it. For years Karen's family has enjoyed the Family Night Tool Chest books by Heritage Builders. These contain family devotions that are anything but boring! Often they include an object lesson or science experiment that portrays a biblical truth. Her family even went to a secondhand store to purchase lab coats to wear during their Sunday experiment times. If you'd like more information on holding a weekly family time, visit www.famtime.com.

MYSTERY TOURS

These are special trips that tie in a verse from Scripture. For example, talk about the verse that reads, "Taste and see that the Lord is good" (Ps. 34:8). Then head to an ice cream parlor for hand-dipped ice cream cones on a hot summer's day.

GREET THE SUNSET

Make a Sunday wreath or banner to hang up each Saturday night at sunset with a prayer thanking God for the day. Or craft your own box for the poor; at sunset on Saturday evening, drop in coins. When the box is full, send the money to a favorite charity or missionary.

WHAT MAKES YOUR SUNDAYS UNIQUE?

Try different things to make Sundays stand out as special days.

Serve chocolate only on Sundays, or any other food that your family loves—maybe it's raspberries, or maybe dill pickles!

Connect with other Christians worldwide. Use Sunday afternoons as a time to read about persecuted Christians around the world who can't attend a church service of their choice as easily as we can. A great resource for this is Voice of the Martyrs; more information can be found at their website, www.persecution.com. They have many wonderful projects for your family to link up with, such as Blankets of Love, a program to send blankets to the persecuted Christians of Sudan.

Make music, even if you can't sing. Let the kids in your home learning to play an instrument try their hand at a hymn or contemporary Christian song. Have worship music on CD playing in your home. Sing Sunday school songs with the little ones. God just said to make a joyful noise; He didn't say anything about it having to be in tune!

Reward a job well done. Now is the time to reward the children for bad habits broken, verses memorized, or anything else they have been working on. Just as the Jewish father blessed his children each week, use Sundays to encourage yours as well. Stickers, trinkets, and small treats are a delight to little ones on Sundays and serve as an incentive for working hard on the tasks at hand.

Use Sunday-only dishware and make meals more formal. One of us found an entire set of gold-edged white china at an estate sale for five dollars!

Be sure to go to church anticipating being God's hands and feet to someone that week. Take the Crock Pot Challenge. This is where you go to church not knowing who you will invite home for Sunday dinner, just that God has someone in mind for you to share a meal with that week. Rotate who gets to suggest a person or family each week. Have your kids be on the lookout for someone who had a rough week or could use a little cheering up. Here are some recipes to get you started. Happy Sunday!

Kelly's Herbed Pot Roast

1 sirloin tip roast (3–3½ pounds), frozen	½ teaspoon pepper
1 teaspoon salt	1 10½-ounce can condensed beef broth
1 teaspoon dried marjoram	1 pound bag baby carrots
1 teaspoon dried thyme	8 medium potatoes, peeled and quartered
1 teaspoon garlic powder	1 large onion, quartered

Before going to bed, put the frozen roast in a crock pot. Combine seasonings and sprinkle over the meat. Pour broth over meat. Cook on low through the night. In the morning add the carrots, potatoes, and onion. Continue to cook on low. After coming home from church, enjoy the meal.

Trish's Creamy Chicken and Noodles

This is a tasty dish that is easy to throw into the slow cooker before you head off to church on Sunday morning. Just use whatever is in your pantry to create this creamy comfort food.

1 pound boneless, skinless chicken breasts
1 10½-ounce can cream of chicken or cream of mushroom soup
½ cup sour cream or plain yogurt
½ cup shredded cheddar or mozzarella cheese
8 ounces wide egg noodles

Before leaving for church, place chicken in slow cooker. Season as desired with seasoned salt, pepper, garlic powder, thyme—whatever you like. Then spread soup over chicken and put lid on cooker.

Cook on high for 4 to 5 hours. Then cook noodles as directed on package. While they are cooking, add sour cream or yogurt and shredded cheese to chicken and stir to combine. When noodles are done, drain and add to mixture in slow cooker. Cook for an additional 15 minutes to combine flavors.

Karen's Stuffed Pork Chops

- 8 double cut pork chops, ready for stuffing
- 4 cups dry cornbread stuffing mix
- $1/3$ cup dried tart cherries, chopped
- $1/4$ cup butter, melted
- $1/4$ teaspoon salt
- 1 cup orange juice
- $1/4$ cup honey or light corn syrup

Combine cornbread mix, cherries, butter, salt, and orange juice in a mixing bowl. Stuff pork chops with the stuffing mix and arrange them on the bottom of a slow cooker. Brush lightly with the honey. Cover and cook on low for 8–10 hours or on high for 4–6 hours.

Peanut Butter Fudge Cake

- $1/2$ cup flour
- $3/4$ cup granulated sugar, divided
- $3/4$ teaspoon baking powder
- $1/3$ cup milk
- 1 tablespoon oil
- $1/2$ teaspoon vanilla
- $1/4$ cup creamy peanut butter
- 3 tablespoons cocoa powder
- 1 cup boiling water

In a small bowl, combine flour, ¼ cup sugar, and baking powder. Mix in milk, oil, and vanilla. Add peanut butter and place mixture into slow cooker. In another bowl, blend ½ cup sugar and cocoa powder. Add boiling water and stir until thoroughly combined. Pour slowly over batter in slow cooker. Do not stir. Cover and cook on high 2 or 3 hours or until toothpick inserted in the middle of cake comes out clean. Serve with vanilla ice cream for a delicious end to any meal!

Books of the Bible

When your child learns all the books of the Bible by heart, treat him or her to a special project by making a Bible cake. The child can look up the verses to find the ingredients. This recipe uses the King James Version. After the cake is done, you can all celebrate the accomplishment of reciting the books of the Bible with a delicious treat.

INGREDIENTS:

½ cup Genesis 18, verse 8, word 4

1 cup Isaiah 7, verse 15, word 3

2 Job 39, verse 14, word 4

2 cups 1 Samuel 28, verse 24, word 19

2 teaspoons 1 Kings 19, verse 6, word 10, plus Matthew 21, verse 44, word 22

1 teaspoon Exodus 30, verse 23, word 17

¼ teaspoon Luke 14, verse 34, word 1

¾ cup 2 Samuel 16, verse 1, word 40

½ cup chopped Genesis 43, verse 11, word 44

Judges 5, verse 25, word 12

In a large bowl, soften and cream Genesis 18 with a mixer. Slowly beat in Isaiah 7. In a small bowl, beat Job 39 well and add to creamed mixture. Sift together 1 Samuel 28, 1 Kings 19 and Matthew 21, Exodus 30, and Luke 14. Add to creamed mixture and mix thoroughly. Fold in 2 Samuel 16 and Genesis 43. Grease an 8-by-11½-by-2-inch pan with Judges 5. Pour in batter. Bake 30 minutes at 350 degrees. Lower oven temperature to 325 degrees and bake 15 minutes more or until a toothpick inserted comes out clean. Makes 12 servings.

"Welcome to the Family" Prayer Basket

To celebrate with someone who has recently become a Christian, give them a prayer basket. Fill a basket with the following items:

- a copy of the Bible in an easy-to-understand version
- a journal
- a fountain pen
- a copy of a Bible study or devotional
- some bags of flavored tea or hot cocoa
- a new mug
- some tissues
- some note cards or stationery for jotting notes to a friend they are praying for

Attach a copy of the tag on page 183 featuring 1 Thessalonians 5:16–18. This can double as a memory card as they hide God's Word in their heart.

Bless This House

Home ownership is a big step whether one is single, married, or part of a family with children. This venture not only warrants a celebration but may even be taken a step further and turned into a dedication of sorts. Taking the time to pray not only for God's blessing upon this new home but also for the very people whom He will touch in the future in this dwelling can make this a special time indeed.

If you have friends or loved ones who have recently moved, plan a time to show up at the new residence with a tasty meal in hand. This can either be one made fresh to enjoy right then or one that can be refrigerated or frozen for later use. The following recipe for easy chicken pot pie works well. If frozen, simply thaw and then proceed with the baking directions as written.

For further celebration, take along a Housewarming Basket. In a pretty basket place the following items:

- some change of address cards
- a loaf of homemade quick bread such as banana or pumpkin or a dozen muffins
- some honey-cinnamon butter—simply blend one stick of butter at room temperature with ¼ cup honey and 2 teaspoons cinnamon. Place in a small antique crock or purchased deep dish bowl and chill. Cover with plastic wrap before giving.
- a spreader or antique butter knife
- a wall plaque with a Scripture verse or housewarming sentiment
- a journal or guest book that can be used in the years to come to record signatures and well-wishes from house guests
- an elegant fountain pen to go along with the book

Don't forget a copy of the tag from page 182 that states, "But as for me and my household, we will serve the LORD" (Josh. 24:15).

After delivering the basket, take some time to pray with the new homeowners. Ask God to use this place for His glory to reach others with the love of Christ and for the homeowners to offer as a haven for those whom He brings their way.

Easy Cheesy Chicken Pot Pie

1 box refrigerated pie crusts
2 cups chopped, cooked chicken breast
1 bag mixed vegetables for soup (corn, carrots, peas, and potatoes)
1 can cream of chicken soup
1½ cups shredded sharp cheddar cheese
   salt and pepper, to taste

Bring pie crusts to room temperature. Place one in a 9-inch pie tin. Set aside second crust. Mix remaining ingredients in a large bowl. Place mixture in bottom crust. Top with remaining crust. Crimp edges and prick top of pie with a fork. Using a paring knife, carve out a small heart in the middle of the top crust. Wrap with plastic wrap until time to bake. Bake at 350 degrees for 1 hour. Enjoy!

Mother-Daughter Celebration

YOUNG LADIES' DAY

In explaining their upcoming cycle to my daughters, I decided to make it something to anticipate with joy instead of the obvious "Yuck!" (That would take care of itself.)

Well ahead of the day, we gave it a name, Young Ladies' Day, and decided how to make it special—visiting the lingerie department for some beautiful new underthings, followed by lunch at our favorite sit-down restaurant.

When the day arrived, we did have the initial "yuck," but with the plan already in place, we dropped all usual activities and enjoyed a very lovely and memorable time together. Our chatting was laced with Scriptures about how we are fearfully and wonderfully made. And we ended our lunch laughing over every girl's basic need—chocolate!

Debi Davis, Saint Johns, Michigan

All day long Anne was so excited about her tea party that she could think of nothing else. Marilla helped her plan the menu. Besides tea, they would have fruitcake, cookies, and ginger snaps, with butter and cherry preserves.

ANNE OF GREEN GABLES BY L. M. MONTGOMERY

Celebrate your daughter's girlhood by creating a special time together once a week for tea and sharing. Choose a time each week that is reserved for you and your daughter. Purchase special teacups that are used only during this memorable time. Your daughter will be able to cherish her teacup and put it in her hope chest.

Fill a pretty basket with special teas, cider, honey, and sugar. Then choose a Bible study or character building book that you can share together. Here are some ideas to use in your tea time.

❧ *Beautiful Girlhood* by Mabel Hale. This early 1900s reprint will encourage and help your daughter as she blossoms from girlhood to womanhood. A revised and updated version by Karen Andreola is also available.

- *The Companion Guide to Beautiful Girlhood* by Shelley Noonan and Kimberly Zack. A Bible study used along with *Beautiful Girlhood*.
- *Christy* by Catherine Marshall. A young city girl travels to the hills of Tennessee to teach the poor mountain children. Lessons abound as Christy learns to love the people she meets.
- *A Young Woman After God's Own Heart* by Elizabeth George. A study to encourage young ladies to follow after God's heart and become spiritually strong.
- *God's Wisdom for Little Girls: Virtues and Fun from Proverbs 31* by Elizabeth George. Reading this book with your daughter will let her see the beauty of Proverbs 31 and how she can display it in her life as a little girl.

Priceless—Words to Grow On

Introducing someone to God and His Word could be the greatest gift you ever give. With this mission in mind, a pastor's wife gave her daughter a used Bible on her thirteenth birthday.

That's right: a used Bible.

The mother had bought a new Bible, read through the entire book in one year, and made little "mom notes" in the margins. These notes were written especially from mother for daughter about favorite passages, spiritual yearnings, memories of how a biblical truth was learned, or various people who embodied certain attributes of God.

The Bible was given with a Scripture reading plan to take the daughter through her eighteenth birthday. Not only did the daughter receive insights into her mother's heart but she had a guide for getting into the Word every day until she was on her own.

What better gift could you give to someone in your family than God's Word—and how better to give it than with a testament of your faith in your own words?

The Hope Chest Celebration

In the past, hope chests were a tool every mother used to prepare her daughter for marriage. Inside the hope chest were examples of all the skills and projects that the young lady learned in the years she was under her mother's tutelage. They also included family heirlooms passed down from generations, reminders of precious loved ones.

Young ladies today are missing this important aspect in preparing for their future. Whether a young lady remains single or married, she will most likely one day be a keeper of her home. A hope

Books on Hope Chests

The Hope Chest Legacy: A Legacy of Love by Rebekah Wilson is available online at www.hopechestlegacy.com. This book is a loving mother's collection of historical facts on hope chests and gives many ideas for what goes into a hope chest for each one of your children.

Preparing Your Hope Chest: Building a Foundation of Godly Character for Tomorrow's Mothers by A. B. Leaver is published by Pearables (www.pearables.com). This is another great book, especially for a young girl beginning to put together her hope chest. It gives many ideas and projects for the young lady to make.

chest is a treasured legacy that can be passed down to many generations. While a hope chest party may seem a little old-fashioned in the day we live, it may be just the right celebration for a daughter blossoming from girlhood to womanhood. A hope chest party could be used for a young lady turning thirteen or sixteen or somewhere in between. Or it can be held whenever you feel your daughter has demonstrated homemaking skills in several projects and has collected things for her home. A hope chest party would be a great way to show others her handiwork. Here are some ideas to use for this celebration.

Invite women and friends that have made an impact on your daughter's life so far. As parents, purchase a hope chest as a gift for your daughter. It may be brand new or a refinished heirloom. Or the daughter may want to choose her own. Give this to her at the celebration. Include a gift tag from page 183 that includes 1 Peter 3:3–4. The daughter can display some of the items she has made or collected around the chest.

Have each person bring an item for her hope chest. A gift of love and thoughtfulness means more than the price. Let the guests know what her favorite color is to make gift buying easier. Gifts could be a special bowl, linen, pillow, or recipe. A grandmother or aunt could give a treasured item that is part of the family.

Serve your daughter's favorite refreshments. The mother or a grandmother could share a devotional on Proverbs 31. Pass around a beautiful journal in which each lady can write words of wisdom to the honored guest. The daughter may share what each lady present has meant to her and how each one has encouraged and trained her.

Conclude the celebration in a time of prayer for your daughter, asking that God would keep her pure and protected as she grows into a woman of God.

Purity Covenant

Ron and Pam Sischo of Ovid, Michigan, celebrate with a special tradition on each of their children's sixteenth birthdays. On this special day, Dad takes the child out to lunch at his or her favorite restaurant and presents them with a "promise ring." For their son, it was a simple band of white gold; for the girls, a pearl or diamond. The ring symbolizes a covenant that they prayerfully make together before God.

This covenant is an actual document that they both sign. Dad promises to protect the child from biblically unqualified men/women; to teach the child God's principles of life; and to faithfully pray for the child and for God's choice of a life partner. The child promises to keep himself or herself pure until marriage; to wait for Dad's blessing on any courtship; and to wait for his full release before entering into marriage. The ring, which Dad places on the ring finger of the child's left hand, serves as a constant reminder of this promise between them and God. And the signed and dated document is framed and hung in their room.

To help you develop your own traditions with your young lady or gentleman, here are a few suggested resources:

- *The Heart of the Rose: A Story of Purity* by Mabel A. McKee (available through The Young Advent Pilgrim, www.young adventpilgrim.com). This small book is a reprint of a story written in 1940 and has a wonderful message to young people about the importance of purity and the blessings that come with waiting for the lifelong companion God has for them. Encourages a touching discussion with your young adult.

- *The Three Weavers* by Annie Fellows Johnson. A classic short story written in 1905 and now reprinted for our daughters. This beautiful story illustrates the

AT OUR HOUSE
When Children Are like Little Jewels

When our first child, a daughter, was born, Todd scraped together enough money to surprise me with the gift of a ring set with a small emerald, the birthstone of our new baby girl. He presented the ring to me while I was still in the hospital with Mackenzie, and I wore it until three and a half years later when Mackenzie's brother entered the scene.

Todd had the idea of then getting me a garnet ring, for the month of January, when this child was born. Times were even tighter then and it took Todd until baby Mitchell was nearly a year old to save up the money to buy me a modest, small-stoned ring just like he had when Mackenzie was born. When our second son, Spencer, came along three years later, the garnet ring was replaced by an amethyst one in honor of our son born during a February snowstorm.

I've cherished these inexpensive but heartfelt gifts as I've worn them for the past thirteen years. However, I never dreamed the delight I would have when my husband carried out the next step of his plan. . . .

When our daughter turned twelve, he had that emerald resized to fit her finger. He then took her out on a date, ending up at a favorite swing in a local park in our small Midwestern town. He recalled to Mackenzie the day she was born and how, when she and I were safely snoozing in our hospital room after the hard work of bringing her into this world, he had gone into town to pick out a birthstone ring. He told her of the joy it had been watching her grow, learn, fail, and succeed on her way to becoming all God intended. He also spoke of God's plans for her future and the mate He might someday have picked out for her.

At times choking back tears and at other times letting them go, he told her of his own journey beginning many years ago when Christ was not a part of his life and ending with his conversion at age nineteen and then meeting me, his future wife, at age twenty. He then gave her the ring and told her to take and wear it only if she were willing to commit to remaining pure until her wedding day, the day on which Todd will remove the ring from her finger and give her hand in marriage to the man God has chosen for her.

It was a special time for both of them and to this day she only removes her purity ring to shower. It serves as a constant reminder to her of God's plan for her purity, a plan that began the first day of her life when she lay in her bassinet while Todd scoured the jewelry store looking for just the perfect ring. We're not sure what we will do with the rings that were purchased when the boys were born. We may give them to their wives someday, or perhaps to their daughters if they have any. Or maybe I'll just keep them for myself to serve as a visual reminder to pray for the wives He has chosen for them.

Karen

responsibility of the father in guarding his daughter's heart until marriage. A wonderful story for a father to read to his daughter.

- *The Princess and the Kiss: A Story of God's Gift of Purity* by Jenny Bishop. This is a princess story all children should hear. A king and a queen save a special gift for their newborn daughter: her first kiss. A companion study guide is also available called *Life Lessons from the Princess and the Kiss* at www.reviveourhearts.com.

Coming of Age in the Lord

Then our sons in their youth will be like
well-nurtured plants.

PSALM 144:12

There comes a time when a young boy reaches the season in his life to begin putting childish things away and becoming the man God desires. This time of spiritual maturity is often called "coming of age in the Lord." Parents can celebrate this occasion by giving the gift of a special recognition dinner in honor of their son.

When your son turns twelve, begin sharing with him the areas in his life you want him to be looking at to help him with his growth in becoming a young man. These areas could include salvation, daily spiritual disciplines, character qualities, basic principles of loving the Scriptures, faith, humility, love, and purpose.

As your son approaches thirteen, or when you see him ready spiritually, set a date for a special celebration. Send out invitations to family and close friends and prepare your son's favorite meal. After the meal select a few Christian men your son respects to share some godly words of wisdom that he will keep for years to come.

Finally, have the father share his heart with his son on how God has brought him into your family, what he has meant to you, and some cautions and hopes. He could present his son with a Bible with highlighted verses to encourage him in his spiritual growth and walk with Christ. This would certainly be a cherished gift.

Another idea is to have each guest coming to the ceremony bring a tool that could represent a character quality that the young man will need to possess as he enters manhood. For example, for orderliness, a tool chest could be given; for persistence, a hammer; for fairness, a level. As the person gives the gift he could say a little about the tool and the character quality along with how the Lord has used it in his life. His father could give a large toolbox to the son with a special plate inscribed with the event, date, and a Scripture verse. Or use the tag on page 182 that includes the verse Psalm 84:12.

A related book you might want to get is *Raising a Modern Day Knight: A Father's Role in Guiding His Son to Authentic Manhood* by Robert Lewis. It helps fathers guide their sons to be chivalrous, godly men. This great book includes lots of Scripture, illustrations, and personal experiences for young men—and dads too.

Pamper Body and Soul

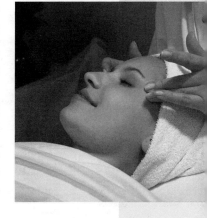

Do you and your friends need a time of rest and relaxation, a time of renewal and refreshment in both your physical and spiritual lives? Unwind with a get-together for two or twenty of your closest friends. Complete with facials, manicures, chocolate, prayer, and reflection, this could prove to be a special time of fellowship and encouragement that none of you will forget.

Send out the invitations provided on page 182. Just put a check mark and an amount next to the ingredient(s) you would like each person to bring—ingredients you'll need to complete recipes for Gentle Oatmeal Facial Masks, Heavenly Hand Cream, and Soothing Scented Bath Salts (recipes follow). You provide whatever essential oil you'd like to scent the recipes. Lavender is a very restful scent.

Prepare your home for a time of restful relaxation by lighting lots of candles. Have plenty of seating available and worship music or hymns softly playing in the background. Have chocolate candies in pretty crystal dishes placed strategically around the room. Have hot water available for flavored hot cocoa or chamomile tea. Make some chocolate-covered fruit for the ladies to sample at their leisure (a recipe follows).

Slice some cucumbers for your facials. In a slow cooker on low heat, place enough damp washcloths for each person. These will be enjoyed when it comes time for the facials.

When the guests arrive with the requested ingredients, spend some time together whipping up the following recipes for Gentle Oatmeal Facial Masks and Heavenly Hand Cream.

Have each guest who would like a facial take a warm washcloth out of the slow cooker. Then have them relax and cover their faces with the cloths for 10 minutes. This opens the pores and softens the skin, which will allow the facial mask to do its work.

Give facials and hand massages! Smooth the Gentle Oatmeal Facial Mask over the skin. Use cucumber slices to cover the eyes while the mask is setting up. Others could be giving each other hand massages with the Heavenly Hand Cream.

Pray for each other as you give the hand massages—if you are comfortable, pray out loud for the recipient, her family, and her life circumstances. Then switch. Leave plenty of time for relaxation and conversation too.

Have guests spend some time alone or in small groups of two or three meditating, discussing, and praying about verses from the Bible on rest and what that means.

Come together at the end of the evening to share and pray about all you have learned and experienced.

Finally, make Soothing Scented Bath Salts for each one to take home and enjoy—and remember to take time to relax.

Chocolate-Covered Fruit

1 10-ounce package white chocolate chips
1 10-ounce package semisweet chocolate chips
2 tablespoons vegetable shortening
   assorted fruits

Place white chocolate chips in one bowl and semisweet chocolate chips in another. Add 1 tablespoon of shortening to each bowl. Place white chocolate chips in microwave and melt slowly, stirring often. Then do the same with the semisweet chips. Dip your assorted pieces of fruit into the different kinds of melted chocolate as desired. You could use strawberries, grapes, banana chunks, apple slices, kiwi slices, pear slices—whatever you wish. Then lay on wax paper and refrigerate until the chocolate hardens. Serve on a beautiful crystal platter or pretty china plate.

Gentle Oatmeal Facial Masks

1 cup oatmeal
1/2 cup plain yogurt or buttermilk
1/4 cup honey

Using a food processor or blender, finely grind the oatmeal until a fine powder is formed. In a bowl, combine yogurt or buttermilk and honey. Blend in oatmeal powder. Mix thoroughly until a smooth paste forms. Smooth over face and neck. Let sit for 15 minutes and then rinse with warm water.

Heavenly Hand Cream

1 cup table salt

1 cup sea salt

1 cup olive oil

a few drops of essential oil (lavender is very relaxing)

In a large bowl, stir together all ingredients. Rub a generous amount onto your hands and gently massage for a few minutes. Then rinse with warm water.

Soothing Scented Bath Salts

For each person, you'll need:

¼ cup Epsom salts

¼ cup sea salt

1 or 2 drops essential oil (lavender is very relaxing)

a quart-sized reclosable bag

a small jar with tight-fitting lid (½ cup capacity)

Have each person place the Epsom salts and sea salt in a reclosable bag. Shake until well combined. Add a drop or two of essential oil; seal the bag and shake again. Open the bag and check the concentration of the essential oil. If the salts don't smell strong enough, add one drop at a time and shake well until desired scent is achieved. Pour in jar, and with a length of ribbon, secure the tag from page 182 onto the rim of the jar.

9

CELEBRATE THE EXTRAORDINARY EVERYDAY

· · · · · · · · · · ·

RAINY DAYS AND ROAD TRIPS, BEDTIMES AND BOOKS

This is the day the LORD has made;
let us rejoice and be glad in it.

PSALM 118:24

Our lives hold so many ordinary days full of work, school, groceries, and appointments. Yet just when routine can threaten to overwhelm you, look back on some of the days that might have been routine as usual . . . and then something extraordinary happened. As we look back on some of those days that began with the usual routine, we see that some were transformed into days full of warm memories and nostalgic reminiscences that we can savor in years to come. What's the difference? Why are some days dull and dry while others seem to stand out in our memory, bright and brilliant, as we recall time spent relaxing with friends or conversing with family? When we take the time to enjoy the people we're with in whatever circumstance we find ourselves,

some amazing recollections result. Here are some ideas to get your creative juices flowing—to make each day special!

Rain, Rain, Go Away

For those days when your children clamor to go outside but the weather just isn't cooperating, these supplies can help you make memories. Keep them on hand!

Chocolate, vanilla, and butterscotch pudding make great finger paints! Just use wax paper for a canvas and let your kids make an edible mural.

Playdough, either store-bought or homemade, is a great thing to have on hand and get out for special occasions. Have a laminated placemat for the child to use as a work surface.

Kool-Aid Playdough

- 1 cup white flour
- 1 cup water
- 1 tablespoon vegetable oil
- ¼ cup salt
- 2 tablespoons cream of tartar
- 1 package Kool-Aid drink mix

Mix ingredients in a small saucepan. Cook and stir over medium heat for 3–5 minutes. Soon a ball will form in the center of the pan. Remove from heat. Cool until just warm to the touch. Knead on a lightly floured surface. Store in an airtight container.

Coffee filters and food coloring—who knew these could make the most incredible creations? Butterflies! Just drop a few drops of food coloring onto the coffee filters. Place these outside in the rain for a few minutes. The color will bleed through the filter, creating beautiful designs. Then bring the filter inside and let it dry. Finally, just take the filter and gather it in the middle. Place this section in the head of a clothespin with your amazing designs showing through as the wings.

Beat the Winter Blues

Whether it rains or snows where you live, you can beat the blahs and inclement weather of winter. Try the following.

BLAZE A TRAIL

If you live in a part of the country where you encounter a large amount of freshly fallen snow, it can serve as an avenue for ministry. Grab the kids and your snow shovels or snowblower and head out for an afternoon of clearing driveways. You may want to call your church for a list of shut-ins or elderly folks who might need some assistance. Maybe your neighborhood also includes individuals who would benefit from this service.

WARM A HEART

Another creative way to serve during a heavy snowfall is to head out to a local nursing home. Have your children make snowmen outside the windows of the residents, complete with top hats and carrot noses. Or make snow angels along the outside of the building where the residents can see you. It will delight their hearts and transport them back to the time when they were young and did the same thing.

PLAN A POOL PARTY

On snowy days Susan Sopek of Bloomington, Illinois, turns up the thermostat for a tropical feel and gets on the phone to invite friends and neighbors to her "pool party." A small kiddie pool filled with just a bit of warm water is set up in the living room (on top of plastic garbage bags for splashes), and nostalgic beach music is played in the background. Guests have fun playing beach volleyball with balloons and delighting in a picnic. Make sure everyone invited wears their swimsuits—under their snowpants!

Sick Days

> But his mother made him some hot broth instead, and put him to bed in his cigarette box with a doll's hot-water bottle against his feet. Even so, Stuart caught a bad cold, and this turned into bronchitis, and Stuart had to stay in bed for almost two weeks.
>
> *STUART LITTLE* BY E. B. WHITE

These ideas can make sick days pass more smoothly—and convey all the love and concern you feel. Never underestimate the power of good wishes and how even small acts with great love can be a powerful prayer.

At Our House

TLC: Just What the Doc Ordered

When my husband and I were newlyweds, we knew there would be some differences in how we did things. Older couples would laughingly joke about having debates over how to squeeze the toothpaste or which way to place the toilet paper on the roll. For us, these issues were easy—we had the same opinion on them all. What I wasn't ready for, however, was the way my husband handled being sick.

About four months into our marriage I came down with a terrible case of stomach flu. I thought it was strange that when it first came on in the middle of the night, my husband stayed in bed. A while later I tried to waken him and desperately exclaimed, "I've got the flu!"

"Okay, what do you want me to do about it?" he replied.

What did I want him to do about it? I could think of plenty! When I was growing up, my mother took the opportunity to greatly pamper us when we were sick. We were allowed to rest on the couch, watch television, and sip our favorite soda (something she rarely bought). When we were feeling a little better, we were even allowed to eat on that couch, a true no-no on normal days. And when we had to use the bathroom to be sick, mom would be there to hold our hands and offer a cool washcloth for our heads.

My dear husband, however, had a very different experience and expectations. He and his four siblings had a mother who was a nurse for forty-three years. Their home was run much like a hospital: kids in separate rooms, buckets by their sides, instructions to ring when the buckets were full, food delivered by rounds on schedule each day, and no whining allowed!

Fortunately, now that we are parents of three children ourselves, we've resolved our sick day differences, determining that the best approach is probably somewhere between his experience and mine—but always with plenty of tender loving care.

I think I may be converting my husband, though. The last time he was under the weather, I asked if there was anything I could do. He smiled sheepishly and said, "Well, now that you mention it, some Stewart's Key Lime Soda does sound good . . ."

Karen

Bring relief and cheer with a "Get Well Basket" filled with tissues, lemon drops, a can of chicken noodle soup, a good book or magazine to read—anything you can think of to help soothe and heal.

Borrow books on tape from the library for children who are bedridden but otherwise alert enough to be bored. Introduce some classics like *Charlotte's Web* or *Stuart Little*, both by E. B. White. For older children try *The Chronicles of Narnia* by C. S. Lewis or *Christy* by Catherine Marshall.

Dedicate certain items for "sick day only" to make an ill child feel special—for example, a "Get-Better Bear" or a sick-day plate, cup, or bowl featuring a favorite character or in a favorite color.

Make Special Day pillowcases for a sick loved one (see instructions on page 161). These should be made out of soft flannel to provide the ill every possible comfort.

Pull out the board games for kids ill enough to be home but starting to go stir-crazy. Karen's kids enjoy playing Pit and Scrabble with their dad using the actual games that he had when he was a child. For younger ones, playing easy card games like Old Maid and Go Fish alone with Mom and Dad make them feel especially grown up.

Play hospital. Copy the "medical chart" on page 174 and place it on a clipboard. Then keep a record of the child's fluid intake, how many cups of chicken noodle soup they consumed, and what medications were taken and when. Deliver flowers or a card to your patient. When the patient is feeling better, give them their discharge papers and allow them to change out of their hospital clothes!

If the patient is feeling up to eating, be creative in what you serve. When Trish's husband was sick with chicken pox, Karen's family actually brought over a Lemon Poppy Seed Cake, only they called it Chicken Pox Cake!

Go ahead and pamper. Let the sick person choose their favorite flavor of pop or request a flavor of crackers or soup. A favorite juice or treat would be especially appreciated!

Bedtime Rituals

A little planning and creativity can close an ordinary day with extraordinary memories. Children and even teens seem to open up as soon as they crawl into bed or once the lights are dimmed and they finally wind down to slumber. The following bedtime rituals can make that transition to sleep easier and build fond memories for the years to come; they can also knit you more intimately with your children's hopes, fears, struggles, and dreams.

ASK JUST THREE QUESTIONS

When tucking in your little ones or bidding older children goodnight, ask three questions and wait for what might be a lengthy but important time of sharing: What was the highlight of your day? What was your low point? How can I pray for you for tomorrow?

CREATE A DIFFERENT KIND OF BEDTIME STORY

Instead of the traditional book before bedtime, make up your own tale. If you have multiple children in one bedroom and Mom and Dad both doing the tucking, it may make for quite an adventurous or even silly story. Each night a different person starts. Then take turns going around the room and adding to the story. Some stories are action-filled and carry with them an element of suspense, so much so that they must be continued the next night! Others are so crazy that the whole family ends up on the floor in laughter! It's a delightful way to end the day and make memories with your kids. Who knows? Someday in the future when you are tucking in your grandchildren they may say, "Hey Grandma, tonight you start the story!"

SING TO SLEEP WITH A HEAVENLY LULLABY

Remember how a lullaby could soothe your baby to sleep? A hymn can just as sweetly send older children off to sleep. Each child can have their favorite standby. Every night while tucking, sing one verse of the hymn to him or her. This teaches them the hymn, and they are sure to treasure the words to it as they hear it in the future. You may also wish to research the story behind the writing of the song. Many of them have wonderfully inspiring and sometimes heart-wrenching stories of just how they came to be written. You may change songs after a year so that by the time your child reaches adulthood, they will know a great many of these hymns by heart!

A great resource to help in this endeavor is the book *Hymns for a Kid's Heart* by Bobbie Wolgemuth and Joni Eareckson Tada. In addition to telling the story behind the writing of different hymns, a CD is included to help kids hide these words in their hearts.

INVITE ANGELS TO YOUR BEDSIDE

Kirk and Kelly Weaver of Littleton, Colorado, have a way to teach their children of God's love and protection at nighttime. They have photocopied sketches of angels—not cute, cherub-faced, sweet-looking angels but bold, brave guardian angels—which they use in a clever way. When their children are sleeping at night, they come into their room to pray for them and for God's guiding and protecting hand to be on their lives. They ask Him to send His angels to surround their children and be with them as they go about their day. After they pray, they place a few of the angels up on the wall, varying the place each night. When their kids awaken in the morning, they are met with a very visual reminder of their parents' prayers and God's protection in their life!

Hit the Road in Style

When Heidi found out about the journey, she became so excited she could hardly eat a thing. She was not sure whether she was really awake or just dreaming. But when Sebastian brought down her trunk, she knew everything was real.

Heidi by Johanna Spyri

Road trips are often exciting at first, but they can quickly become tedious as you wait for the next stop! "Daddy, are we there yet?" can get old pretty quickly. Bring along these items to help you cope:

Books on tape will make the travel time go so much quicker! Invest in some or check some out from your local library. Look for *Adventures in Odyssey* radio shows or classics such as *Where the Red Fern Grows* by Wilson Rawls or *Old Yeller* by Fred Gipson.

A book about your destination can be discussed—learn where you're going and what you'll see.

Healthy snacks like carrot or celery sticks, dried fruit, nuts, or even popcorn can stave off hunger when you need to make those extra miles before a meal. Keep special treats for crossing a state line or marking each hundred miles.

Physical games for rest stops like Frisbees, balls and gloves, and badminton can help you get in some exercise and get out some energy.

A roll of quarters for each child can buy you some peace—literally. Each time there is any grumbling, fighting, or horseplay, one quarter is forfeited; the rest can be used to purchase souvenirs.

Travel pillows are great—for everyone but the driver!

Activity books and colored pencils or crayons can keep kids busy.

Disposable cameras—give one to each child to record the trip from his or her viewpoint!

My Two Front Teeth

When your child loses their first tooth, celebrate the big day by taking them out for a chocolate malt. The straw should be able to easily fit through the opening left by the missing tooth!

Read All about It!

In Karen's small Midwestern town, the public library has a policy of allowing children to be issued their very own library card when they reach the age of six. For all three of her children, this day has been quite a cause for celebration. They travel to the library on their actual birthday—bringing the camera to preserve the memory for years to come.

The librarian takes their personal information from them: name, date of birth, address, and so on. Then they receive their very own official library card. No longer do they have to put the books and videos they check out on Mom and Dad's card. They can proudly carry their own in their little purse or wallet. Being responsible for not losing their card makes them feel very grown up and teaches them to be careful. They now have the task of making sure they have no overdue library books and of paying the fine if they do!

To further celebrate the day, Karen prepares a special dinner complete with homemade alphabet soup (alphabet-shaped pasta can be found in most grocery stores) and Dirt Cake with bookworms! (See the recipe for Dirt Cake on page 113.) You may also be able to find ABC shortbread cookies at the department or grocery store. One family she knows even invited one of the librarians over for supper on the day their daughter got her library card. Finish off the evening by allowing your youngster to read one of the books they chose out loud to the family. Happy reading!

Half-Birthdays

Here's a great excuse for mom and dad to get time alone with each child: celebrate each child's half-birthday. Simply figure out the day that their half-birthday is on, which is six months after their real birthday. If their birthday is May 14, then their half-birthday is November 14. Mark this special time with a night out at a favorite restaurant, a movie, or a round of putt-putt golf. Any reason is good enough to spend the evening together!

Upon returning home, celebrate with the rest of the family by enjoying half of a birthday cake. You can easily make one by baking one layer of a round cake. Use the remaining batter to make cupcakes and freeze for a later treat. When done, cool and remove from pan. Using a long serrated knife, cut the cake in half. Use frosting to stack the two pieces on top, forming half a birthday cake. Spread the remaining frosting on the top and sides of the cake.

Date Your Mate

You'd be amazed at how a little time and attention, just like when you first dated, can keep your marriage energetic and loving. Practice these ideas and look for the difference!

One day each week Pam Sischo of Ovid, Michigan, and her husband plan a Date Day—usually over a lunch hour. This allows them to spend much-needed time alone without children or telephones to interrupt. "I enjoy this time where I am able to sit across the table from my husband, studying his face as I have since we first dated some twenty-nine years ago," Pam says. It also helps the Sischos stay in sync. They always bring their date books and fill each other in on their personal schedules for the coming week: meetings, activities for the kids, church events. "This is when we will resolve

any conflict in our schedules," Pam says, "and that makes the coming week, and ultimately our marriage, run much smoother."

Pizza and a Movie Night helps Susan Sopek of Bloomington, Illinois, and her husband keep the fun in their marriage. They order pizza (or make frozen ones), spread towels on the family room carpet for a picnic blanket, and watch a movie. "This is the most fun during the winter when it's dark out early," Susan says. "It's like going to a drive-in (with a closer bathroom!). Bath towels are easier to clean up than a large blanket and are more absorbent than sheets, just in case there are any spills!"

Enjoy the outdoors as well as time with your loved ones—take in the park, walk down the driveway or around the block. Join your son for an exploring expedition in the woods. Spend time with your daughter strolling through a zoo. You don't need an agenda. Time spent together makes for great conversation and unforgettable memories.

Bon Voyage

Do you know someone who's about to embark on a journey across the sea? Why not throw them a Bon Voyage Dinner?

Think about their destination. What foods can you come up with that will give them a small taste of what's to come? Are they traveling to England? Why not make fish and chips? How about Mexico? An authentic Mexican meal would hit the spot. Is Hawaii their next stop? Try making Pineapple Upside Down Cake (recipe follows) to give them a taste of the islands before they even leave home.

Pineapple Upside Down Cake

1   8½-ounce can sliced pineapple, drained but with juice reserved
3   tablespoons margarine
½   cup brown sugar
⅓   cup vegetable shortening
½   cup sugar
1   egg
1   teaspoon vanilla
1   cup flour
1¼ teaspoons baking powder
¼   teaspoon salt

Melt 3 tablespoons margarine in an 8-by-8-inch pan. Mix brown sugar and 1 tablespoon of the reserved juice into the margarine. Arrange pineapple slices on top of this mixture. Add enough water to remaining pineapple juice to make ½ cup of liquid.

In a large bowl, beat shortening and sugar until light and fluffy. Add egg and vanilla and mix well. In a smaller bowl, mix together dry ingredients. Add alternately with pineapple juice to shortening mixture, blending well after each addition.

Spread batter over the pineapple slices. Bake at 350 degrees for 40 to 45 minutes.

Off to College

When Billie Busch of Beverly Hills, Michigan, sent her son off to college, she wanted him to be prepared. She purchased a large, off-white, drawstring canvas bag and had his initials monogrammed on one side in large type. (You could cut letters out of fabric and adhere them to the bag with fusible web, like Wonder-Under, available by the yard at fabric stores.)

The bag would be used for laundry, Billie knew, but to start she filled it with dryer sheets, a stain stick, a roll of quarters, and tablet laundry detergent.

"The bag doesn't take up nearly as much space in a dorm room as a laundry basket would," Billie says, "and is much easier to carry to the washing machine!"

BACK HOME NIGHT

"Rejoicing hearts are treated to the dear familiars of home when our sons burst through the door for a college break," says Debi Davis of Saint Johns, Michigan.

"The next chapter of the current read-aloud book reserved for the entire family awaits, with warm tapioca pudding on the stove to soothe the homesick tummies. No new recipes are in order for this special family night—it's only the 'dear familiars' we all long for."

Make your son or daughter's visit home from college a special one. Revive an old family ritual, make the bed in their room with special pillowcases, and pull out a "You're special" plate at dinner time.

100 Days!

To beat the midwinter blahs and re-infuse some energy into the year, Shawna Shaw's family in Grand Ledge, Michigan, goes all out celebrating the one hundredth day of school.

"We eat one hundred pieces of cereal for breakfast," she explains, "hotdogs cut into one hundred pieces for lunch with one hundred grapes, one hundred oyster crackers, and one hundred M&M's for dessert; we have hot chocolate with one hundred marshmallows in it for an afternoon treat while the kids each work on the new one-hundred-piece puzzle that they are given as a gift that day."

Other ideas: try reading one hundred books (collectively) on this day! Or, if you homeschool, have one hundred minutes of school. What fun!

Building Family Memories with Books

But no matter how many books Heidi read, the one that Grandma gave her was always her favorite. She read it over and over and kept it in a special place in her room. When she returned to the mountain, she would read it to Grannie.

Heidi by Johanna Spyri

You can travel so many places around the world and venture back in time, all from your living room couch. Reading times are for cuddling, wrapping up in blankets, and sipping hot cocoa in winter or lemonade in summer.

"Nothing brings a family together like a good book," Kelly confesses. "My children probably won't remember all the books we read, but I know they'll cherish our time together enjoying great literature—and they'll remember that feeling of exploring the world together."

Make family reading time a ritual. Find a time that works best for your family. Maybe it's before naptime or after the kids come home from school and while they're eating homemade cookies. After dinner might give everyone incentive to clear the table and do the dishes speedily. Of course, bedtime can be the perfect time for a good book to settle everyone down.

Try to read aloud to your children every day. Choose classics that have stood the test of time and contain characters with high morals.

Finding a good book is important. There are many sources for finding good books, and Gladys Hunt's book *Honey for a Child's Heart* is filled with wonderful recommended readings. Kelly says, "My well-worn copy has been used over and over for finding just the right book for our read-alouds. You know it's a winner when you finish a chapter and they say, 'Just one more chapter, please!'"

Whatever works for your family, make every effort to take time away from the business of life to build memories reading with your children. Couples can do this too. Many famous married couples, like Sheldon Vanauken, author of *A Severe Mercy*, and his late wife, Jean, would read great novels to one another. Some friends have Saturday morning breakfasts and read-aloud times—a different kind of book club meeting. Be as creative as you want with books. They will always take you places!

Make Any Day Special

You did your usual morning walk in half the time? One of the kids earned an A on a particularly tough test? Someone earned a raise? You can celebrate anything by deeming it "special," and these ideas can help.

SPECIAL DAY PILLOWCASES

So many different kinds and prints of fabrics are available nowadays, something for every occasion. Why not take advantage of this to make pillowcases for every special occasion? Kids especially love pillowcases designated for special days and honors. Here are the instructions in eight simple steps:

1. Purchase 1 yard of fabric in whatever print you choose. Look for fabrics featuring holiday and seasonal prints, birthday cakes, or a motif that is special to your child—maybe their favorite animated character. Be sure to use a soft flannel if you're making one for a sick day!
2. Wash, dry, and iron the fabric.
3. Cut the fabric into a rectangle 40 inches wide and 35 inches tall.
4. Fold the rectangle in half width-wise to make a rectangle 20 inches wide and 35 inches tall, with the finished side of the fabric folded in, right sides together. Press.
5. Using a straight stitch, sew a ½-inch seam across the bottom and up the long side of the rectangle. Turn right side out and press.
6. Fold the top of the pillowcase under ½ inch and press. Then fold under again 4 inches and press. This makes that nice fat fold you see on store-bought pillowcases.
7. Sew close to the fold line around the outside edge of the pillowcase, almost 4 inches in from the top of the pillowcase.
8. Let your special loved one enjoy your handiwork!

AT OUR HOUSE

Serving Others with the Special Plate

We use a Special Day Plate to commemorate our children's spiritual birthdays. On the anniversary of the day they accepted Christ as their Savior, they get to eat on an "I Am Special" plate.

After the evening meal we always celebrate with a heart-shaped cake, celebrating when they asked Jesus into their heart.

Then, instead of a traditional gift, they get an envelope with one dollar for every year they have been in Christ—and they must think of a way to use this money to bless someone else. The idea is to offer someone something undeserved, which is the definition of grace.

We've bought flowers for neighbors, put the money in a baby bottle for a pregnancy care center, bought toys for needy children, and given to missionaries at church. What we've received is even greater: joy and renewed understanding, one spiritual birthday at a time, of the meaning of grace.

Shawna Shaw, Grand Ledge, Michigan

THE BLUE (OR RED OR . . .) PLATE SPECIAL

Begin a tradition in your family of using a Special Day Plate, a time-honored tradition in early American families. Many times early Americans celebrated by serving dinner on a red plate to the family member who deserved a special praise or attention. Your plate can be any color or type you like, but make it one you only bring out for a special person on a special day.

The special plate can help you celebrate birthdays, awards at school or church, acts of kindness, half-birthdays, or just for the love of it. Parents can also get in on the fun by celebrating anniversaries, birthdays, Mother's Day, and Father's Day with the plate.

Let the honored person choose their favorite meal, lead the prayer, and be the first to be served the food.

Whatever the occasion, a Special Day Plate will make everyone feel honored and loved. These plates make a wonderful wedding gift for your children when they marry so they can start their own tradition. You can buy red plates that say "Special" in many gift stores or online, or you can create your own using an old-time favorite like a Make-A-Plate kit or by writing in your own hand on an unusual plate with permanent markers (Sharpie makes these in many colors now).

SPECIAL DAY DOOR HANGERS

Anytime you want to acknowledge an achievement or occasion in your home, use our "You're Special Today" door hanger featuring Zephaniah 3:17, "He will take great delight in you, he will quiet you with his love, he will rejoice over you with singing."

Simply photocopy the door hanger on page 175 and adapt it with your own decorations, or even use it as a pattern to cut out of felt (which you can buy in sheets at craft stores or large discount stores like Wal-Mart). The next time someone in your family needs a quick pick-me-up or a "well done!" place this on their door knob for the day.

FRESH FLOWERS FOR NO REASON

Never underestimate the power of the little touches that can show your family how much you love them. A little effort goes a long way in spelling out just how special those living under your roof are to you.

Do you purchase fresh flowers only for anniversaries, birthdays, or your Valentine's Day centerpiece? If your kids see a beautiful bouquet adorning your dining room table, do they suspect that company's a-coming? It is time to change your thinking.

Why not celebrate your family life with fresh-cut flowers for any and every reason—instead of maybe just a few times a year, how about most any time of year? Did your third-grader who struggles with spelling just bring home his first A on his weekly test? Did your preteen daughter save the volleyball game with an incredible eleventh hour spike? How about the three-year-old who slept at Grandma's all night for the very first time?

This needn't be expensive or call for exotic flowers. It could be that you grab a bouquet at the grocery store or cut some branches from a shrub or tree in your yard. Even tall grasses can make beautiful arrangements. Experiment and be creative.

Use the small card provided on page 183 to congratulate the family member whose accomplishments you commemorate. Place the card in a prominent place for all to see.

SPECIAL BIRTHDAYS OF FAMOUS PEOPLE

A fun way to turn an ordinary day into a special one can be to celebrate the birthday of a historical figure. Some possible examples follow, but use your imagination. Who would be of particular interest to your family? Do a little research and then come up with some creative ways to celebrate the anniversary of their birth! Here are a few to get you started:

Wolfgang Amadeus Mozart's birthday was January 27. Mozart is a famous composer from the eighteenth century. His father, also a musician, taught him to play the harpsichord, violin, and organ before the age of six. His playing was so superior that he was asked to perform before royalty. He composed his first piece of music at the ripe old age of five. His life, although cut short, brought us many beautiful songs to enjoy for all time. On the anniversary of his birthday, put on some of his music or take in a concert. Perhaps you could take your children to the home of a pianist who would show them some of his music and play it for them too.

Thomas Jefferson's birthday was April 13. The third president of the United States was important in our nation's history. Check out a book about his life or memorize some interesting facts about him. Did you know that he was fluent in not only English but also French, Latin, Italian, Spanish, and Greek? See if you can do a little research and learn how to say "Happy birthday!" in any one of these languages.

Johnny Appleseed's birthday was September 26. Known to settlers of Pennsylvania, Indiana, and Ohio in the early 1800s as Johnny Appleseed, John Chapman was an interesting fellow. His speech and dress were rather odd, but settlers welcomed him and his mission to plant apple trees

HALF PAST EIGHT

A Reminder of Just How Quickly the Days Fly By

Dear Lord, where has the time gone? It's already half past eight. It seems just a minute ago the clock read one or two.

Just a while ago, my child, you were so tiny, so fragile, and there was so, so much to do: midnight feedings, endless rocking, learning to do all a new mother must do. I was scared. So were you—your tiny little fingers curled around mine—but we learned together, you and I, and the clock kept ticking.

Every tick, every tock, passed slowly, I thought then. I couldn't wait to see you talk, then to walk, but each day seemed an eternity. And then your personality began to emerge. You cooed "dada" and strung together random words like a priceless string of pearls. What queen could buy these treasures?

First steps: "Oooohh"—Boom!—"Get up and keep going, honey!" First dresses: "Mommy, I pretty!" "Yes, you are, my sweet." Your first pony ride: I walked so close. You clung so tight. Before too long you begged me to let go. "Okay, honey, but just for a moment."

Everyone from doting grandmas to complete strangers told me how very quickly time would fly, but for me it seemed to march slowly on.

The clock soon struck three. Peter was there. And Flopsy and Mopsy and Cottontail too. So many hours we spent with them, curled up in that old oak rocker. We left them only briefly, to visit with others. Do you remember? Pooh and Piglet, Papa Small, and Curious George. They were our gang each afternoon before I lay you in your bed. You were too big by then for your crib. And besides, a new baby bundle of brotherly blue had taken over that corner of your room. "Shhh . . . baby's sleeping. We'll read one more and then off to bed, my lamb. It's nearly half past three."

The cuckoo clock cheerfully announced the arrival of four. With it came many new adventures. Your first trip to the dentist (you were very brave), staying all night at Grandma's (how many cookies did you eat?), and Sunday school, birthday parties, and on and on and on. No sooner had the cuckoo tucked back in and shut his wooden doors when the chimes rang out five times.

Is it five already? Where has the time gone? The chimes brought with them lace and frills and everything pink. We then spent our afternoons chatting over tea.

wherever he went. He traveled by foot, clearing fields and woods and planting apple seeds. Later he would return to make sure that all was going well with the young seedlings and to teach others how to care for the trees. Honor his memory by taking a trip to an apple orchard or researching just what particular type of apple he may have planted. What kind of apple seeds did he place in the ground so many years ago? Today we have many new varieties available to grow. Finish off your celebration by whipping up a delicious dessert made from apples. For a few possible ones to try, see page 64.

Louisa May Alcott's birthday was November 29. Louisa, a tomboy just like the character Jo in *Little Women*, spent her childhood in Boston and Concord, Massachusetts, where she was inspired by visits to Ralph Waldo Emerson's library. She started her career as a writer by penning poetry and short stories that appeared in many magazines of her time. When Louisa was thirty-five years old, her Boston publisher, Thomas Niles, requested that she write a book for girls. The result was *Little Women*, a novel based on Louisa and her sisters' growing up years. Take time today to read *Little Women* or *Little Men* aloud, or start several weeks before and end your reading time on the anniversary of her birthday. Have the children in your family take a crack at writing their own short stories or pieces of poetry.

Pooh and Piglet still visited at times, though not quite as often. For the most part they were replaced with a newfound friend. Remember? She met us in the old oak rocker faithfully each day. It was Laura. And Mary. And Carrie. And even that mean old Nellie Olson. Oh, how you loved their world! Your curls were replaced with two long braids; your pink with gingham blue (it was Laura's favorite too). You wore that old bonnet strung down on your back and would answer only to "Half-pint." "Pa called Laura that," you'd insist. So we churned butter and baked biscuits and I learned to answer to "Ma!" (What happened to "Mommy"?) No time to question. Just look at the time . . .

Six . . . and then seven. Maybe they were right. Time marched more quickly. You no longer needed me for books. Now you could read by yourself! And often you did as that baby bundle of blue turned into a toddler who simply adored his Big Sis. So we journeyed to the library and got reacquainted with Peter and friends. You introduced them to your brother, who now occupied your lap. "One more time, sissy, please, just one more!" he would plead. "Okay," you'd answer. "But just this once, brother. It's getting very late." Oh, darling, if you only knew.

And now here we are at half past eight. Who knows what you'll be at the stroke of twelve? The stork came again. Again he brought blue. "Two brothers. How wonderful!" came your reply to the news. This one came to rest happily upon your left hip. And there he remains perched as you now go about your day. Mixing dough in the KitchenAid (what happened to your plastic play stove?) and answering the phone (what about the toy one with the curly cord you dragged behind you all those years? Where is it now?).

You've come so far, my baby. From scribbles on scrap paper mailed to loved ones far away to now answering emails (will you show me how to use it sometime?); from ribbons and smocked dresses to bobbed hair and bell-bottoms. Sometimes I feel as if I'm peering into a mirror from long ago. "Your whole life is ahead of you!" strangers say to my girl. But not for me—for me time speeds by.

Help me make the most of this hour, Lord. I can never live it again. Just look at the clock on the wall. I'm afraid for this mom it is getting very late. Slow the time down, dear Lord, please.

It's already half past eight.

Karen

10

Make the Finishing Touches

. . . .

LABELS AND TAGS, CERTIFICATES AND COUPONS

Now finish the work, so that your eager willingness to do it may be matched by your completion of it, according to your means.

2 Corinthians 8:11

Many of the gifts and party ideas presented in this book wouldn't be complete without a special gift tag, certificate, invitation, or reminder. We have provided everything you need for the perfect finishing touch right here! Just take this book to your local photocopy store. Copy whatever pages you need to complete your special memory onto light-colored card stock paper. Cut out and incorporate in making your day extraordinary.

Here are some simple ideas to make your tag or certificate beautiful:

- Check your local craft or scrapbooking store for papers with interesting colors and textures.
- Cut out the photocopied tags, certificates, and invitations with decorative-edged scissors. You could even use Mom's old pinking shears.
- Use chalk, colored pencils, watercolor paints, or markers to add color to tags and invitations.
- Add accents like buttons, charms, ribbon, and trim that can be glued or even sewn on paper.
- Using double-stick tape, secure the tag or reminder to a darker coordinating color of paper. Try layering two or more colors, leaving anywhere from $1/8$ to $1/2$ inch of the darker color showing beyond the border of the light-colored card stock.
- Laminate special certificates you'll use year after year with clear Con-Tact paper.

THE WISE AND THE FOOLISH

Verse	Wise	Foolish
Proverbs 10:8		
Proverbs 10:23		
Proverbs 12:15		
Proverbs 15:5		
Proverbs 15:20		
Proverbs 21:20		
Proverbs 29:11		
1 Corinthians 1:18		
1 Corinthians 3:18–20		

The fear of the LORD is the beginning of wisdom; all who follow his precepts have good understanding.

Our Family's Prayer List

Pray continually; give thanks in all circumstances, for this is God's will for you in Christ Jesus.

1 THESSALONIANS 5:17–18

To Our Dear Dad

"Honor your father . . ."—which is the first commandment with a promise—"that it may go well with you and that you may enjoy long life on the earth."

EPHESIANS 6:2–3

With love,

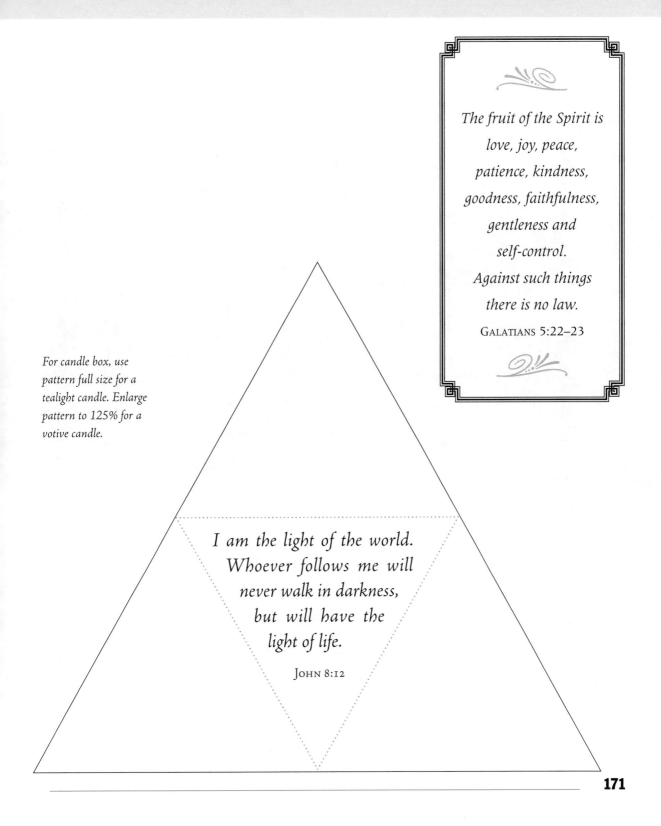

The fruit of the Spirit is love, joy, peace, patience, kindness, goodness, faithfulness, gentleness and self-control. Against such things there is no law.

GALATIANS 5:22–23

For candle box, use pattern full size for a tealight candle. Enlarge pattern to 125% for a votive candle.

I am the light of the world. Whoever follows me will never walk in darkness, but will have the light of life.

JOHN 8:12

For the Lovely

_____ is patient,

_____ is kind.

_____ does not envy,

_____ does not boast,

_____ is not proud.

_____ is not rude,

_____ is not self-seeking,

_____ is not easily angered,

_____ keeps no record of wrongs.

_____ does not delight in evil, but

_____ rejoices with the truth.

_____ always protects,

_____ always trusts,

_____ always hopes,

_____ always perseveres.

1 CORINTHIANS 13:4–7

WANTED!

Name: _____

Age: _____

Height: _____

Hair color: _____

Eye color: _____

Chocolate milk moustache on upper lip.
Last spotted riding a rocking horse west of town.

Please come help us capture this varmint. Once we have the outlaw
in custody, we'll rustle ourselves up some grub and
celebrate cowboy style! Please send wire telling us if you can come.
Until then, partner,
Yee haw!

Date: _____

Time: _____

Location: _____

Please RSVP to: _____

_____

_____

by _____

Medical Chart for:

_____

(Name of Patient)

Age: _____ Weight: _____ Height: _____

Symptoms: _____

_____

_____

Temperature: _____ Time Taken: _____

Medication: _____

Time Taken: _____

Fluid Intake: _____

Time Taken: _____

Food: _____

Time Eaten: _____

Date of Discharge: _____

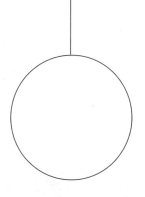

Your big day is here at last...

HAPPY BIRTHDAY!

Choose what you'd like for your special breakfast:

_____ **Bacon**

_____ **Cereal**

_____ **Eggs**

_____ **Fresh fruit**

_____ **French toast**

_____ **Ham**

_____ **Pancakes**

_____ **Potatoes**

_____ **Sausage**

_____ **Toast**

_____ **Yogurt**

_____ **Waffles**

_____ **Orange juice**

_____ **Chocolate milk**

Other: _____

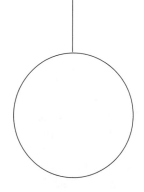

. . . .

you're Special today!

He will take great delight in you, he will quiet you with his love, he will rejoice over you with singing.

ZEPHANIAH 3:17

. . . .

I have set my rainbow in the clouds, and it will be the sign of the covenant between me and the earth.

GENESIS 9:13

Noah brought the animals two-by-two,
Now to my party, I want to bring you!
We'll eat and play and have some fun,
And make our own rainbow before the party's done!
Please let me know if you'll attend—
I hope to see you there, my friend!

Party for: _____

Date: _____

Time: _____

Location: _____

Please RSVP to: _____

_____

by _____

See!
The winter is past; the
rains are over and gone.
Flowers appear on the
earth; the season of
singing has come.

SONG OF SONGS 2:11–12

And she gave birth to her firstborn, a son. She wrapped him in cloths and placed him in a manger, because there was no room for them in the inn.

LUKE 2:7

Come help us celebrate the birth of our Savior!

Date: _____

Time: _____

Location: _____

Please RSVP to: _____

_____

_____

by _____

Jelly Bean Prayer

Red is for the blood He gave.
Green is for the grass He made.
Yellow is for the Son so bright.
Orange is for the edge of night.
Black is for the sins we made.
White is for the grace He gave.
Purple is for His hours of sorrow.
Pink is for our new tomorrow.
A bag full of jelly beans,
colorful and sweet,
A prayer, a promise,
a small child's treat!

The Candy Cane

A candy maker in Indiana wanted to make a candy that would be a witness, so he made the Christmas candy cane. He incorporated several symbols of the birth, ministry, and death of Jesus Christ.

He began with a stick of pure white hard candy: white to symbolize the virgin birth and sinless nature of Jesus, and hard to symbolize that He is the solid rock foundation of the Church and the firmness of the promises of God.

The candy maker made the candy in the form of a *J* to represent the precious name of Jesus, who came to earth as our Savior. It could also represent the staff of the "Good Shepherd," with which He reaches down into the ditches of the world to lift out the fallen lambs who have gone astray.

Thinking that the candy was somewhat plain, the candy maker stained it with red stripes. He used three small stripes to show the stripes of the scourging Jesus received, by which we are healed. The large red stripe was for the blood shed by Christ on the cross so that we could have the promise of eternal life.

Unfortunately, the candy became known as a candy cane, a meaningless decoration at Christmas. Or is it?

Pass along the tale and show that the candy maker's meaning is still there for those who have "eyes to see and ears to hear."

Author unknown

Consider how the lilies grow. They do not labor or spin. Yet I tell you, not even Solomon in all his splendor was dressed like one of these.

LUKE 12:27

Oh! The things which happened in that garden! If you have never had a garden, you cannot understand, and if you have had a garden you will know that it would take a whole book to describe all that came to pass there.

THE SECRET GARDEN BY FRANCES HODGSON BURNETT

You are invited to a . . .
Garden Party!

Come prepared to enjoy the fruits of the season.
Wear your favorite floral prints and a straw hat or flower in your hair.

Date: _____

Time: _____

Location: _____

Please RSVP to: _____

_____

by _____

Lavender Cookies

1½ cups flour
2 teaspoons baking powder
½ teaspoon salt
½ cup butter
1 cup sugar
1 teaspoon lavender
    blossoms

In a small bowl, combine flour, baking powder, and salt. Set aside. In a larger bowl, cream together sugar and butter. Add lavender blossoms and stir until well blended. Add in flour mixture and stir until combined. Drop teaspoonfuls onto ungreased cookie sheets. Bake at 375 degrees for 8 minutes or until lightly browned. Delicious!

It is love that marks a true
daughter of the King.

HEAR YE! HEAR YE!

Her Majesty, Princess _____

of the house of _____

requests your presence at the birthday celebration

of the _____th year of her birth, at our castle (location)

_____

on (date) _____

at (time) _____

Please RSVP to Queen and King

_____

_____

by _____

The angel said to the women, "Do not be afraid, for I know that you are looking for Jesus, who was crucified. He is not here; he has risen, just as he said. Come and see the place where he lay."

MATTHEW 28:5–6

Come Help Us Celebrate

the Birthday of Princess

_____

Love . . . comes from a pure heart and a good conscience and a sincere faith.

1 Timothy 1:5

Date: _____

Time: _____

Location: _____

Please RSVP to: _____

_____

_____

by _____

*Love . . .
comes from
a pure heart
and a good
conscience
and
a sincere
faith.*

1 TIMOTHY 1:5

Please help us to celebrate with the birthday girl by coming to her Un-Slumber Party! We'll have pizza and snacks, play games and have fun, but will NOT sleep! Come dressed in your sleeping best anyway! Pajamas, curlers, teddy bears, and other stuffed toys are welcome. Bring your sleeping bags and pillows too so we can bed down for the last part of the party to visit and have fun . . . but NO SLEEPING ALLOWED!

Birthday girl:_____

Date: _____

Time: _____

Location: _____

Please RSVP: _____

_____

Gone Fishin'?

Gone Fishin'

Join us for a "Reel" fun time celebrating

_____'s birthday!

Date:_____

Time:_____

Location:_____

Please RSVP:_____

_____

"COME, FOLLOW
ME," JESUS SAID,
"AND I WILL MAKE
YOU FISHERS
OF MEN."

MATTHEW 4:19

_____

Therefore put on the full armor of God, so that when the day of evil comes, you may be able to stand your ground, and after you have done everything, to stand.

EPHESIANS 6:13

_____

CALLING ALL SOLDIERS OF GOD TO HELP CELEBRATE

_____'s birthday!

Date:_____

Time:_____

Location:_____

Please RSVP:_____

_____

Thank you ...

"I thank my God every time I remember you" (Phil. 1:3).

There is a time for everything, and a season for every activity under heaven.

ECCLESIASTES 3:1

. . . .

Just for the Bride!

For:_____

Date:_____

Time:_____

Location:_____

RSVP to:_____

Help us to get the bride off to the right start by giving her an Around-the-Clock bridal shower. Please bring a gift that she can use during the time of day listed below. See you then!

_____ a.m. or p.m.

The True Meaning of the Candy Cane

White is for my Savior
Who's sinless and pure!
"J" is for Jesus, my Lord,
   that's for sure.
Turn it around
And a staff you will see.
Jesus my shepherd
Was born for me!

—AUTHOR UNKNOWN

Recipe:_____

_____

From the Kitchen of:_____

Ingredients:_____

_____

_____

_____

Directions:_____

_____

_____

_____

You're Invited!

Date:

Time:

Location:

Please RSVP to:

Taste and see that the Lord is good; blessed
is the man who takes refuge in him.

Psalm 34:8

You're invited to an
In-the-Kitchen Bridal Shower!

For:_____

Date:_____

Time:_____

Location:_____

RSVP to:_____

For your gift, please choose something that can be used in a kitchen for preparing
one of your favorite recipes. On the enclosed recipe card, share that favorite recipe
with the bride-to-be!

RASPBERRY-PEACH

FREEZER JAM

Store in refrigerator or freezer.

Relax—Revive—Refresh—Renew

You are invited to share in a time of restful relaxation!
Please bring the following item(s) marked:

_____ cups oatmeal

_____ cups plain yogurt or buttermilk

_____ cups honey

_____ cups table salt

_____ cups sea salt

_____ cups olive oil

_____ cups Epsom salts

"Find rest, O my soul, in God alone; my hope comes from him" (Ps. 62:5).

O LORD Almighty,
blessed is the man
who trusts in you.

PSALM 84:12

SOOTHING SCENTED BATH SALTS

"Find rest, O my soul, in God
alone; my hope comes from him"
(Ps. 62:5).

Add ¹/₄ cup salt to warm,
running bath water.

But as for me
and my household,
we will serve
the Lord.

JOSHUA 24:15

*Blessed is the man who fears
the LORD, who finds great
delight in his commands.*

PSALM 112:1

Congratulations!

You did a great job!

Your beauty
should not come from
outward adornment. . . .
Instead, it should be
that of your inner self,
the unfading beauty
of a gentle and quiet spirit,
which is of great worth
in God's sight.

1 PETER 3:3–4

Give me neither
poverty nor riches,
but give me only my
daily bread.

PROVERBS 30:8

**Create in me a clean
heart, O God, and
renew a steadfast
spirit within me.**

PSALM 51:10 KJV

*Be joyful always; pray
continually; give thanks in
all circumstances, for this
is God's will for you in
Christ Jesus.*

1 Thessalonians 5:16–18

**Keep me as the apple
of your eye; hide me
in the shadow
of your wings.**

PSALM 17:8

PERSONAL DATES

My record of birthdays, anniversaries, and other dates to celebrate and remember.

January

_____   _____
_____   _____
_____   _____
_____   _____
_____   _____
_____   _____

February

_____   _____
_____   _____
_____   _____
_____   _____
_____   _____
_____   _____

March

_____   _____
_____   _____
_____   _____
_____   _____
_____   _____

April

_____
_____
_____
_____
_____
_____
_____

May

_____
_____
_____
_____
_____
_____
_____

June

_____
_____
_____
_____
_____
_____
_____

July

_____   _____
_____   _____
_____   _____
_____   _____
_____   _____
_____   _____
_____   _____

August

_____   _____
_____   _____
_____   _____
_____   _____
_____   _____
_____   _____
_____   _____

September

_____   _____
_____   _____
_____   _____
_____   _____
_____   _____
_____   _____
_____   _____

October

November

December

INDEX

ACKNOWLEDGMENTS

Our heartfelt gratitude to so many who continue to encourage these three Michigan moms in their publishing journey:

To our friends and fellow laborers at Hearts at Home national ministry as well as the many MOPS (Mother's of Preschoolers) groups we are privileged to have been a part of: thank you for giving us a forum where we can share our ideas and passion with other mothers just like us.

To the dozens of women who sent us their original ideas that now adorn the pages of this book: thanks for letting us step into your homes to get a glimpse at the many ways you build memories with your families. Our special thanks to Debi Davis. What an awesome example you are of a mother with a plan to celebrate even the everyday. Thank you for sharing your creative ideas with moms everywhere!

To our wonderful family at Revell Books, including our marvelous editor, Jeanette Thomason: for the hours of editing, proofreading, marketing, and management, we are forever grateful!

And of course to our own dear husbands and children: thanks especially to YOU for being the objects of our affection as we celebrate within our four walls everyday. We love you!

Finally and most of all, to our Father in heaven: for sending your Son Jesus who invites us to attend the greatest celebration ever planned—eternal life with You in heaven forever. Mere words could never express our true thanks.

ABOUT THE AUTHORS

These three Michigan moms began Homespun Gifts from the Heart workshops six years ago for churches and women's groups including Mothers of Preschoolers International (MOPS). Collectively, they've taught in public schools as well as at home; contributed to magazines; won sewing, quilting, and cooking awards; served as pastor's wives; counseled youth; taught Bible school; coached cheerleaders; created women's events (deep breath) . . . but not all in the same day!

Karen Ehman admits she's the "hopelessly craft-challenged one" in the trio, though she enjoys baking and cooking and has won several blue ribbons at various county fairs. She's a graduate of Spring Arbor University, the wife of Todd, and the homeschooling mother of their three children. As a frequent speaker to moms' groups, Karen is a regular contributor to the monthly magazine and devotional of Hearts at Home, served for five years as the editor of *A Mother's Mission* newsletter, and has been a workshop leader at regional and national mothers' conferences every year since 1997. Before motherhood, Karen was a teacher, cheerleading coach, and pastor's wife.

Kelly Hovermale, the craft queen and natural seamstress of the group, is Westland Michigan's 1999 Mother of the Year. With a master's degree in elementary education, she taught third grade for several years before marrying Greg; she now homeschools their three sons and one daughter. She is passionate about challenging women to weave literature into their gift-giving ideas and is active in the homeschooling community, serving as a speaker and mentor. She's also the former editor of the Creating Family Memories section of *A Mother's Mission* newsletter.

Trish Smith loves to work on the computer and inspired her friends to make this book with the adorable gift tags and labels she adds to the countless handmade gifts she makes for family and friends. Before marrying Doug and homeschooling their son, Trish attended Western Michigan University and worked in the floral and fabric industries. Today she spends much of her time with children: teaching homeschooled girls to sew, leading a Boy Scout troop, and coordinating craft time for her church's Vacation Bible School. In her spare time, she loves listening to and making music, sewing, quilting, crafting, and finding ways to make her home a haven for her family.

"PRACTICAL, FUN, & INSPIRING."

Elisa Morgan,
president and CEO,
MOPS International

Whether you're glue-gun challenged or a craft queen,
Homespun Gifts from the Heart will help you create
more than 200 gifts—from candy cane cappuccino
to windowsill gardens.